INSPIRATION IN ACTION™

A WOMAN'S GUIDE TO HAPPINESS

KATHIE DONOVAN

...Helping You Create the Life You Desire

Text copyright 2013 by Kathie Donovan, Queen Bee Productions.

All rights reserved. Except for a reviewer who may quote brief passages in a review, no part of this book may be reproduced, stored in a retrieval system or transmitted in any form or by any means without the prior permission in writing of the publisher Kathie Donovan.

Inspiration in Action is a registered trademark of Kathie Donovan.

www.kathiedonovan.com   1-877-718-4869

ISBN 978-0-9918822-0-5

Published by Kathie Donovan, Queen Bee Productions.
Printed in Canada.

Are you disconnected from the whispers of your heart?

Do you feel unworthy of happiness?

Have you unwrapped the divine gifts that you've been given?

Life is precious and feeling happy is your birthright.

We make ourselves available to embrace the abundance around us when we centre on being grateful and have the courage to step into the truth that we are spiritual beings having a human experience.

Inspiration in Action *will change the outcome in your life as you discover how to co-create with the law of attraction using some amazing power tools.*

Believe and receive.

Preface

I am sincerely grateful that you have chosen to share this journey with me. The principles in this book have been a great support on my path to happiness; I hope they will be helpful for you too. This book is intended as a guide; in no way is it a replacement for therapy or counseling.

Some of the content will challenge what you think you know, so I encourage you to have patience with yourself as you explore. I strongly suggest using the pages at the end of each chapter to write down ideas that come to you as you practice the exercises. Keeping track of how our thinking shifts over time can be very empowering; seeing it in writing sends a strong message to our inner critic and produces a powerful result.

Foreword

"Isn't life just freakin' amazing?"

From across the room, around the corner or with my back turned, I'd smile and nod. I'd know those words anywhere. And I'd know it was Kathie Donovan speaking them.

In an Oprah-centric, self-help happy world, it seems there are many "teachers" ready to inspire us to live more, do more, be more. Whether it's Dr. Phil or Dr. Wayne Dyer, they want us to reach inside and truly be present, within ourselves and in the moment.

No doubt, they all have their gifts. But I don't know them as I do Kathie. And I certainly don't know their journey.

A few years ago, Kathie and I met for one of our regular breakfasts at a local greasy spoon diner. We laughed, old friends that we are. We swapped news. And we discovered we were on the same path, spiritually speaking. Without having discussed it, we'd both been reading *The Secret* by Rhonda Byrne.

It's funny how one idea can galvanize change. As Kathie described her thoughts about the law of attraction, her eyes lit up and she practically wiggled in her seat. On that day, our bond deepened and broadened into an exquisitely kindred touchstone.

To see Kathie in action as a TV producer and journalist, you can understand the intersection between people and their true selves. With more than 35 years in broadcasting – many of them with CTV's Ottawa-based show *"Regional Contact"* – Kathie focused her trained eye on ordinary people doing extraordinary things. She would draw them out, cast them in the brightest light and celebrate them in every way she knew how. Anyone who knows her – and those reading this book soon will – could see her tender heart, shining soul and role as a motivational teacher emerging.

Of course, the culmination of her gifts is this gift to us: *Inspiration in Action: A Woman's Guide to Happiness.* Through it, Kathie urges us to have courage. She shows us that thoughts of forgiveness or a simple act of kindness can have unseen, but positive waves of influence upon others. And she teaches that if we affirm who we truly are, we have it within ourselves – each of us – to stand in the spotlight of our own stage and sing our song to the world.

But most of all, through *Inspiration in Action*, Kathie reminds us of one simple and utterly undeniable fact: **life is freakin' amazing!**

Michelle Valberg
Award-Winning Canadian Photographer

Dedication

"No action misses the mark if its intention is pure."

I woke up one morning with the above statement in my head and thought it characterized this project perfectly.

This work is dedicated to my amazing and devoted husband Kensel Tracy whose wisdom and tender love have helped to heal my heart, nurture my dreams and awaken my spirit.

I am deeply grateful for my friend Michelle Valberg who has been my sister from another mother on this journey.

There are many women who gave of their time and energy to be the research and development team for this book. Thank you for your kindness, your patience and your diligence.

I am grateful for all of the teachers who have given confidence to this project through their inspired actions. I give thanks every day to the angels and the universal energy that guides us all.

Introduction	1
Gratitude: Thank You, Thank You, Thank You	15
Courage	33
Surrender and Release	55
Grace and Illumination	73
Compassion and Kindness	83
Forgiveness	93
Vision Boards	103
Affirmations	109
Boundaries	115
The Mindfulness Project	123
Sharing Inspiration in Action	133
Acknowledgements	141
Contact Information	142

INTRODUCTION

I have asked myself over and over again: *"Who am I to write this book?"* I didn't invent the law of attraction; I didn't even know what it was until about 1996. Since that time, I have studied and practiced co-creation with this law and the results in my own life have been pretty astonishing. In many ways I am a different person because of what I have learned. I want to share my experience in the hope that even one person will be inspired to shift their thinking to get better results.

The Buddhist teacher Thich Nhat Hanh said, "There is no way to happiness, happiness is the way." The title of this book, *Inspiration in Action: A Woman's Guide to Happiness*, is an interpretation of that brilliant quote. Happiness is not a destination, it is a choice. It's a feeling I have as a result of shifting my thinking. Each time I choose peace instead of chaos, compassion instead of judgment and courage instead of fear, I am choosing happiness.

The great contemporary American philosopher and poet Maya Angelou says, "If you learn it, teach it." I discovered in her wisdom why I needed to write this book.

For much of my life, I felt like I was digging around in a big overstuffed purse, trying to locate my happiness. I pulled out all kinds of impractical tools that I attempted to use to produce contentment in my life but none of them worked. Everything I tried offered fleeting gratification until I began a journey that was both frightening and exhilarating.

I wasn't sure if what I was connecting with was the wisdom that comes with menopause or if I was tapping into an inborn intelligence. I have since learned that each of us has this wisdom: a deep knowing that waits for us to remember it. Everything we need to be happy is inside us. Happiness is a choice; happiness is the way.

Since embarking on this adventure, I have come to rely on my intuition. I believe that it is the voice of spirit or whatever you call the power greater than us. The subtle messages of intuition are beautiful moments of guidance that we have to get quiet to hear. I believe in the power of these moments. I also believe in the law of attraction and I believe that we co-create with this powerful force, whether we're aware of it or not. Every thought we think sends a message about what we want to receive. This journey of *Inspiration in Action* is all about making ourselves available to receive what it is we say we want instead of what we don't want.

In learning to shift my thinking, I have created space to receive what I want. I have connected with a feeling of contentment that I nurture every day by choosing my thoughts wisely. I am learning one of life's simplest and most profound messages: when you have an open heart and an open mind, you are open to receiving. I am grateful that I took a risk and listened to the guidance that has brought me here to be with you.

I came home from work one day and told my husband that I was seriously thinking about leaving my job. I loved my work co-producing and co-hosting a top-rated weekly television show. I have always been passionate about communication and making a difference in people's lives. So when the station announced that they were changing the business model and essentially cancelling our show, I knew instantly somewhere in the deepest part of me that a chapter in my life was ending.

You see, my secret fantasy, the one I hadn't shared with anybody, was to leave my job within two years to share what I had been learning about the law of attraction and *Inspiration in Action*. I wanted to show others what happiness looks like so they might be inspired to shift some of their thinking. For a few years, I had been writing ideas for this book in my spare time with no clear deadline. The severance package that the television station was offering would cover me for the two years I would need to work toward my goal. I took a deep breath and made the difficult decision to close the door, so another one could open.

Dream Maker

I was actually stunned that my secret fantasy had come true in this way. I believe in and co-create with the law of attraction every day and I'm still surprised when what I wish for shows up because it's always in an unexpected way and at an unpredictable time. The beautiful thing about the way the law of attraction works is that there's always an opportunity to learn.

I have discovered that something has to shift in order for our dreams to show up. In the moment of the shift, it sometimes feels like something really bad is happening. We ascribe the meaning good or bad to the situation; it is neither.

Something has to shift in order for our dreams to show up. Thoughts that no longer serve our dreams and goals have to shift and sometimes physical situations have to shift as well. It can feel bad or it can feel good and we need to experience that too. Often when we look back we see the situation for what it was: the thing that needed to shift to bring our vision to life. When we co-create with this powerful law, it's clear to me now that in order to be open to receiving, we need to believe in the power of our thoughts and believe in the power of our dreams.

It's the Law

Rhonda Byrne's book, *The Secret*, introduced me to the law of attraction. Simply put, the law of attraction states that what you focus your attention on is what shows up in your life or "as ye think so shall ye be" (Jesus Christ) or "what we think, we become" (Buddha). *The Secret* introduced millions of readers to this powerful law that has apparently been used intentionally or unintentionally since mankind has walked the earth. It has been written about since books have been written. *The Secret* made the law of attraction seem so simple to use: think about something and poof it shows up. Not so fast. There's a lot more involved in intentionally co-creating with this powerful force and that's what I want to explore here.

I read Michael Losier's book, *The Law of Attraction*, and saw him give a fantastic seminar. Michael spoke in great detail about how the law of attraction works and he made the point that we humans are really good at coming up with the list of what we want, but we're not always available to receive.

I experienced an "aha" moment in that seminar and I left excited because I wanted to understand more. Soon I had the germ of an idea for what is now *Inspiration in Action: A Woman's Guide to Happiness*. I wanted to start a research group to explore the concept that Michael had presented. I wanted to figure out how I could make myself more available to receive and how I could be of service to others.

My brilliant friend Michelle Valberg offered her photography studio as a place to meet and between us we invited nine other women to join the mission. Each one of the women had indicated that they were interested in exploring the law of attraction; I felt that we needed that in common. I didn't want to have to work to convince anybody of what was becoming clearer to me. The group met once a month for close to two years and in that time we explored together what are now the principles of this program. We all planted seeds for our dreams and many of us are living those dreams today.

Inspiration in Action: A Woman's Guide to Happiness is called a woman's guide because it has been my guide. The principles relate to anyone willing to be open to receiving more in their life: more abundance, more joy, whatever it is your heart desires. I call the principles of this program "power tools" because I believe they are effective devices that we can rely on to keep us heading in the right direction.

Inspiration in Action is about working with the law of attraction to co-create and it's about shifting thoughts and feelings to become more available to receive. Practicing the principles of *Inspiration in Action* shifted my thinking from a lack mindset to an abundance mindset. It made me more aware of mindfully sharing my abundance with others: sharing love, time, money, whatever I have an abundance of. At the end of the book, I have compiled a list of simple exercises called *The Mindfulness Project* to encourage and challenge each of us to share our gifts with others.

I have always thought of myself as a very lucky person and now I realize that what I called luck was actually the law of attraction bringing my dreams into physical form. I had unknowingly co-created a lot of wonderful situations, including meeting the man of my dreams and establishing a successful career in broadcasting. I had also co-created a lot of drama that in many ways kept me stuck. I began to understand that using this power intentionally and mindfully would allow me to create better results in my life. Getting to know more about the law of attraction helped me to appreciate that the only person whose life I can really influence with my thinking is my own.

Malcolm Gladwell talks about how little things can make a big difference in his book, *The Tipping Point*. If you create a shift in your thinking and I create a shift in mine, that's two people added to thousands more, working their way toward creating a better outcome for themselves and for the rest of the world. Eventually the numbers become so great that a shift is created: a shift in consciousness that affects us all. I felt that Malcolm's observation answered another question – why bother? What difference can one person make? Well, if thousands of people shift their mindset, not only will each of us benefit, we'll benefit as a collective too. Win, win baby.

Happiness Found

While many of us are working on how we can improve our lives and have a positive impact on this world, North American society has experienced a shift in the other direction as well. We are more plugged into our electronic devices than we are to each other. We seem to be searching for happiness everywhere but where it lives. Many of us think we'll be happy when we get a new job, a new boy/girlfriend, lose weight or purchase the latest cell phone or hottest designer bag.

The ego or storyteller, as Dr. Jill Bolte Taylor calls it, will keep us searching forever if we try to find happiness that way. In her book, *My Stroke of Insight*, she talks about the functioning of the right and left brain. The left brain is home to what she calls our ego, our protector or our storyteller. She says the ego is always looking for one of three things: it wants to be right, it wants to feel special or it wants to be miserable. Once we feed it what it wants, it's immediately hungry again and the search continues. I love how my thinking mind/ego protects me and I understand now that it's not where happiness is found. The simple truth is that happiness is a feeling that we already have; a feeling that we have lost touch with because of all of the distractions in our world.

More than ever, we are infatuated by celebrity. We want to look like the people we see on the red carpet and we want to live like them too. What we don't want to see is the reality that they're people just like we are with zits and hair extensions, great fitting Spanx® and sometimes suffering in their heart. We want to believe their public relations; we connect with the show business of their business. We don't get to see the talented hair and makeup people and the lighting team. We know it's all an illusion, but we buy it anyway. It's a great distraction from the challenges we all face that might be painful or uncomfortable. I'm not judging anyone for how they choose to spend their time, I'm simply suggesting that we are far too comfortable under the spell of this illusion and it takes us away from our own possibilities.

Many people feel marginalized for a variety of reasons: everything from perceived limitations to the messages we identify with in the media, like the ones I mentioned above. These messages are intended to make us feel that we are not enough, that we need a new mop to feel whole and good enough. We are so manipulated by clever marketing that some of us feel it's impossible to measure up. We'll never be enough if we listen to the external messaging and not the internal whispers because what we've simply forgotten is that we are fine just the way we are in this moment.

We seem to pay less attention to the life in front of us and more attention to either what is yet to come or what happened in the past. What kind of life are we living when we're constantly competing, judging and dismissing, beating ourselves up about perceived past mistakes and living in fear of what the future "might" bring?

The simple truth buried beneath all of the anxiety that is so prevalent in North America today is that we are lost and we need to find ourselves – literally find ourselves.

The Search

For years, I lived in my head instead of in the flow of my life. I lived in fear and regret: fear about what the future held and regret around all of the mistakes I thought I had made in the past. I felt deep shame as a child; I was tough on myself and even tougher on others. In some twisted way I also knew that I was blessed, even special, although I couldn't for the life of me work out how. I realize now that I had to be with those feelings until I learned about the possibilities of my life. I now believe that each of us is in a unique situation on this life path with individual lessons to learn, plenty of room to grow and great reward when we do.

The concepts of forgiveness and compassion were entirely foreign to me. There was no room in my closed-off and shame-filled world for tenderness of any kind, although I craved it and looked everywhere outside of myself for it. You'll see as you continue that my search was fruitless. My portal to compassion, kindness and forgiveness opened when I began to let go of the mistaken beliefs I held as a result of observing the world around me as a child. The investigation is ongoing; the more I release, the more compassion and tenderness I have toward myself and others.

A shift has taken place in my life since plugging into the principles of *Inspiration in Action*. I now know what happiness feels like. I get that it's not dependent on whether or not I measure up to anyone's standard or whether my closet is organized. It's not about anything external in my life – it's about what goes on inside with my thinking and my feelings. It's defined by how I choose my thoughts.

What are You Willing to Give Up to Receive?

I was a smoker for many years and when I look back, I can't believe that I had the strength to give up that addiction. Smokes were there night and day, through stress at work, bad boyfriend breakups and lonesome evenings when I lived on my own. When smoking became unfashionable, I was one of the last holdouts among my friends. I didn't want to change. I felt comfortable with my cigarettes. Then one day, not long before I got married, I made the decision that I wanted to live a long and healthy life with my true love and I started taking the steps that would get me where I wanted to go.

Man, I think giving up cigarettes is one of the hardest things a human being can do. As impossible as it was to imagine my life without cigarettes, it's impossible now for me to imagine my life with them. Today I can focus on how beautiful the world is instead of being forced to focus on cigarettes. I am grateful for that; I recognize now that in the process of ridding my life of the addiction, I created space for new and healthier habits and I finally began to feel empowered.

Toxic behavior was a thread running through my life. As a young woman, I chose boyfriends who, generally speaking, were not interested in committing. They were nice guys who made their intentions clear up front. They would explain that they didn't want to become attached or make any kind of commitment and I would agree, thinking that once we got a little further down the road they would change their mind.

Of course when that didn't happen, I would cry a river of tears over the perceived loss and now looking back, I see that I chose a no-win situation. I felt victimized in many areas of my life; I couldn't understand why these unfortunate experiences kept happening to me. I wasn't engaged in living, I was engaged in suffering through the behavior I chose. As a teenager, I smoked, I drank alcohol, I experimented with drugs and I looked for love in all the wrong places. I was a victim of my life and because I was focusing on misery, I attracted all sorts of it. Often though, as was the case for me, we can't be present to why we're attracting what we don't want until we're ready to look at the question of what we do want from this life.

For me, the question "what do I want" surfaced after a miserable breakup with a boyfriend. I was in pain and I knew that something in me had to shift because after years of trying to get others to change I was getting absolutely nowhere. I actually wrote a list of the qualities I didn't like in the men I had been with and started to see that what I really wanted was the opposite of what I had been attracting. From the list of what I didn't want I started a list of what I did want and within about a year I had attracted my amazing husband of over two decades. He is one of the reasons I believe in miracles.

When you're living the life of your dreams, you can look back and see how you got there, but you couldn't have charted the course to get there when you set the dream. We can't and we don't need to know the how. That's the magic; that's one of the big secrets of the law of attraction. The how and the when are not up to us; all we need to know is what we want. In other words, we need to connect with our heart's desire.

On the Air

My broadcasting career started when I was eight years old. I was invited by a friend of my father's to be in the cast of a children's radio program. It was frightening and magical: frightening because I felt that I was in the spotlight and for an eight year old with pretty low self-esteem, being on the radio singing and talking with strangers was extraordinary. As frightened as I was, I connected with it. There was magic in that radio and I wanted to be part of it.

When I was a young teenager in boarding school, I listened to a transistor radio under my pillow every night before going to sleep. There was something attractive and inclusive about the community created through the music and the voices on the radio. The disc jockeys were funny and knowledgeable and made me feel part of something. Those experiences created a bond that has never been broken.

I went to university to study communications and left early because I was quite clear about what I wanted to do. I wanted to chase my dream and find a job in radio. I had no idea how or where I would find it.

I moved from Montreal to Ottawa the year one of the universities was launching the first campus FM radio station in Canada. Through acquaintances, I met with the station's program director who threw caution to the wind that day and invited me to join the on-air staff. It was one of those jobs that didn't pay money but ask anyone who worked there and they'll tell you that they were richly rewarded. I couldn't believe my so-called luck. About a year and a half later, a new commercial FM station was starting and I was hired as a part-time disc jockey.

Within a year another woman and I developed a program that started out as a 15-minute show about the local scene and eventually grew to an hour a day.

It was pure joy. I was living the dream that had sprouted when I was eight and the connection was still as magical as it was when I was a child. I should also mention that at no time along this career path did I have any idea what I was doing. I simply had a knowing that this was my path. I wasn't very good in the beginning either and I am thankful for patient bosses who stood by my best efforts until I wasn't an embarrassment.

When I look back, knowing what I know now, I see that I was working with the law of attraction. I set the dream and believed in it without any doubt. The law of attraction was delivering opportunities and I was saying yes.

Although I didn't openly have any designs on a job in television, my secret fantasy was to take my passion for connecting with people to the next level. Out of the blue, I was invited to join the number one television station in Ottawa to do weather and entertainment reporting. As soon as I took the job, I thought I had made the biggest mistake of my life. I'm sure that my new bosses entertained the same idea. Man, that was a tough time although nobody said that living your dream would be easy.

Twenty-four years later, I can say unequivocally that I had one of the best jobs in television in the country. For 14 of those 24 years, I had the pleasure of co-producing and co-hosting "*Regional Contact*," a weekly half-hour show that was all about connecting the people in our community. My amazing co-host and I worked with a small and gifted team, telling stories about the magnificent people in our viewing region.

We called it heart and soul television because just about every story we aired had an inspiring message of some kind. We celebrated people – folks with solid values and a sense of community who had unplugged from their mobile devices so that they could pay attention to their lives and their dreams. We met artisans, farmers, artists, teachers, musicians, athletes and chefs who had a vision in their imagination. Over the years, I began to see a behavior trend among these people. Many of them had what we call blind faith. Despite their fears, they used courage to stay focused on the belief they had about their dream. Those people were pure inspiration for me and for our viewers.

I have learned that passion resides in every one of us and that its whispers can be difficult to hear over the clutter and noise all around us. I learned that we have to get quiet to hear the whispers of our truth. I learned that believing in a dream isn't enough. You have to feed it with action to bring it to life. We are each in charge of our own successes and failures; we create both with our thoughts and our feelings. I think that's where *Inspiration in Action* was born, the kernel of it anyway.

Believing is Seeing

Another real "aha" moment for me was when I realized that we are in charge of our thoughts. For many years, I allowed myself to live under the spell of what other people thought. Everyone else's agenda more or less ran my program and kept me stuck in many ways. Realizing that I could choose not to accept negativity in myself and other people really set me free. Negative thought patterns are a habit, like smoking, so changing to more positive thinking is simply developing a new habit.

Okay, that sounds a lot easier than it is! As I said earlier, giving up smoking was one of the most difficult things I've done in my life. It was really like giving up a good friend. Shifting our thinking from toxic to tender is no walk in the park either, but it's well worth the effort. I am constantly checking on my thinking and I easily fall into the old habit, but I do it less often and get out of it faster. I have more positive thoughts and feelings now than I've ever had.

I was scared as I embarked on my mission of unplugging from old behavior and relationships that were not giving me the results I wanted. I wanted peace and the behavior and relationships I focused on brought a lot of drama. I have learned from reading and listening to wise people like Anthony Robbins that the only road to success is practice, practice, and practice. He models his life after people he sees as successful, so in my quest I am doing the same. I read books that nurture my dreams, allowing me to connect with like-minded people and those who have gone before me on this path.

Since beginning the shift, I have attracted new energy in the fellow seekers I have met, seemingly out of the blue. Having healthy boundaries means that relationships are more comfortable and as I work on accepting others as they are, I am less attached to an outcome and more available to just simply be in a relationship.

The resolve to being open to receiving what I really want in my life is so strong that I developed this program which will hopefully support anyone who wants to change the results in their lives. *Inspiration in Action: A Woman's Guide to Happiness* is not about adding anything to your life. I'm not asking anybody to "buy" my philosophy or take on more responsibility.

In reality, what the concept does is ask you to remove barriers that prevent you from receiving what it is you really want. When you alleviate yourself of the burden you've been carrying from your past or the anxiety you feel about what could possibly come in the future, you will start to attract what it is you want. You will be open to receiving your dreams in reality instead of leaving them in your imagination, across the barrier of your fears.

GRATITUDE:
THANK YOU, THANK YOU, THANK YOU!

Your mother was right, two of the most important words you will ever say are thank you! Our mothers may have had a slightly different motivation for wanting us to be grateful, but it doesn't matter. What matters is that we learn the habit of being grateful and nurture a feeling of deep appreciation. It's the starting point for this personal renovation called *Inspiration in Action*. We have so much to be grateful for and yet we take so much for granted.

It's pretty simple, but a great place to start is by being grateful for your breath. Think about the fact that you can breathe. Think about your heart pumping blood into the system that keeps your body doing its thing 24/7 while you focus on other tasks. Generally, the only time we think about all of the fantastic support systems that make us up is when something goes wrong. We're surprised when our system fails us and find all sorts of reasons to either blame someone or become a victim of the situation. We forget that this is actually happening to our body, which is part of who we are.

The mind and the body are all part of the same system even though our thinking mind would have us believe that the mind and body are separate. The mind, body and spirit are all one.

When we shift to that awareness and learn to be grateful for everything our body does for us, it will follow that we'll want to take care of ourselves out of appreciation for our body.

We are given gifts every minute of every day if we're willing to see life in this way. Developing a habit of appreciation directs our thinking to the present moment, so that we don't miss what's happening in the now. All the great teachers say that the only power we have resides in this moment. When you think about it, it makes sense. The past has no power because it's gone and the future hasn't happened yet, so it doesn't exist either. We spend far too much of our precious energy focused on past and future. In the process, we are missing the miracles happening right now.

I remember years ago thinking it was pretty silly when one of my teachers talked about saying thank you before his feet touched the floor in the morning. He said thank you to that divine energy (call it whatever you like) for providing a bed and for the gift of another morning. Fresh start, new day, what a gift! Now I do it too and I highly recommend you try it.

How about being grateful for the sun, the clouds, birds, flowers or for being able to see? If you can't see, focus on what you can do. It's this shift in our focus that swings our energy and our vibration to another level. This higher level is where the law of attraction will recognize that this is the energy you want returned to you.

So many of us beat ourselves up about how we look. In the past, I felt bad about how much I weighed and there was shame around how I felt about my body. It wasn't until I started to alter my thinking by shifting the focus to what I am grateful for about my body that everything began to feel better. Now I appreciate everything my body does for me, from typing these words on my computer and taking me into the kitchen to make dinner, to hugging the people I love. I could go on forever.

The gift of this human body is simply miraculous when we choose to see it this way. I encourage you to shift your thinking about your body image and notice all of the fantastic things that being in it can produce. It doesn't matter whether you're able-bodied or disabled, there's a very long list of gifts to be grateful for. Once you shift your thinking to gratitude, you lift a barrier and will start to not only notice how magnificent your body is, you'll begin to want to treat it with the utmost reverence.

Remember that what you focus on with your thinking and your feelings is what shows up in your life. Once you shift to gratitude, the law of attraction can match what you're asking for and deliver more to be grateful for.

Thanks to the brilliant Louise Hay, I have learned to thank my car, which I call Snowbelle, for taking me where I need to go. Yes, I speak to Snowbelle now; we actually have quite a good relationship. She's good to me and I do my best to return the kindness.

Call me kooky, but I thank everything now. I started an experiment in my own little world to see what would happen if I became mindful of saying thank you often. It's been a couple of years and what I have noticed is that I have more to be thankful for and that my practice is influencing people around me to be more grateful too. It's all a matter of what we choose to allow.

You can judge this practice as silly or frivolous and that's fine too. I'm not here to pass judgment on anybody else. I am simply saying that cultivating a grateful mindset has been a fantastic power tool in my life and has brought me more abundance to be grateful for. I'm happy about that.

No Audience, No Show

Think of someone in your life who thrives on negativity. You know the person who criticizes everything and everyone? You can feel the negative energy coming from them. It's exhausting to be around them and there's no way you can influence them to be any other way.

The truth as I see it is that they're not really negative people, they're afraid of something and they use negativity and criticism as a way to protect themselves. Of course, the law of attraction always delivers more to criticize and be negative about because that is what they're focused on and in effect it's what they're asking for.

I have spent my fair share of time around this type of personality and frankly, I have tried every trick I know to dissipate their negativity, to no avail. This is an ego-based activity (remember that the ego wants to be right, feel special or be miserable) so now I call on a technique that I picked up on after years of dealing with a negative and critical mother.

It took me decades to get this but I figured out that if I didn't engage in whatever shenanigans my mother was talking about, there was no negativity because she needed an audience for that. It worked! It worked like magic. So, the expression I used when referring to conversations with my dear Mum was "if there's no audience then there's no show."

I have compassion for people who feel the need to lead with criticism and negativity, but I choose not to engage. I will not allow people who want to argue, be defensive or confrontational to press my buttons any longer. I will stand up to them of course if they confront me, however I won't engage. I will tell them that they're absolutely right, whatever it is they're talking about because that's what they're looking for. So thank you very much, you're right and let's move on.

I should add that the greater challenge for me is to then send love and compassion and thank those people for teaching me something. After all, gratitude is a practice as are all of the other principles of *Inspiration in Action* and I do believe I will practice it for the rest of my days.

Peace Out of Pain

Now think of someone you know who is always positive; someone who never seems to have a bad day. You can feel the energy from them too and if it feels good then that person is someone who is able to appreciate their life and the gifts in it. I bet that person receives a lot of gifts too! Isn't it attractive and energizing to be around someone who is positive? When we focus on the positive, we attract positive energy to us. It's the law of attraction: like attracts like! I've never met a positive person I didn't like!

It seems that some people are born with a positive outlook and some of us have to work to get there. I'm one of the ones who had to work at it. People have always commented that I am a positive person and their perception is correct because my exterior has generally been upbeat. I have always chosen to laugh and smile a lot. When I was younger, what people saw on the outside didn't match what was on the inside. I learned early in life that I would get a better response if I pretended that everything was fine. I also wanted to fit in and how I felt really didn't fit in with anything I saw around me.

While I had a deep knowing that everything was perfect, that I was special and that life would somehow work out, I also had a deep feeling of dread and of not being enough. Looking back now, I can see that my true self was trying to be heard and my thinking mind had a louder voice, so I believed what it told me.

I suffered in silence in that I didn't acknowledge the emotional pain I felt, but my behavior told another story. Childhood for my sister, my brother and me was an unstable experience. My father's job took our family from one coast of Canada to the other, we changed schools and friends and even though our parents did the best job they could, my father was an alcoholic and quite unavailable to us. I was the baby of the family and I looked for attention often by behaving badly. I didn't feel that I had any kind of compass to lead me through life. I just sort of followed whatever felt right to me. I didn't know that other kids had a positive living environment – I thought everyone had the same kind of stressful household. I would learn much later that our mother and father both struggled with depression.

From my early teenage years to my 30s, I found comfort in all the wrong places. I did learn yoga in my late teens and studied philosophy at university in an attempt to connect with the mystery of my spirit. I also used recreational drugs, cigarettes, alcohol and sex to comfort the part of me that was in pain. The distractions helped temporarily, but by the next day the feelings were still there. So guess what? I had to find a way to dull the pain again. What a futile exercise! There was never any peace and all I looked forward to was getting high so that I wouldn't have to feel my feelings.

It wasn't until my 30s that I really had a look at myself and the results I was getting in my life. I realized that I had to take some action if I wanted to shift the results. I had to alter something on the inside so that it would match the outside. That was when I learned about deep appreciation and began the work of developing an attitude of gratitude.

I went to a therapist for a few years and learned there that my parents did the best they could. I committed to discovering what having a healthy relationship was about and I started with myself. I read Sarah Ban Breathnach's book, *Simple Abundance*. In it, Sarah provides a special message about gratitude for every day of the year. I read the book every day and started to notice that I was available to appreciate the events, people and even the small things in life a little more. I took the focus off of the inner drama and started shifting my awareness.

Then, inspired by Oprah Winfrey's habit, I started keeping a gratitude journal beside my bed. Each night before I went to sleep, I wrote down five things that I was grateful for that day.

I would write at the top of the page:

Today I am grateful for:
Having a house to live in
Having healthy lungs
Having a husband who loves me as much as I love him
Having two sweet kitties
Having the resources to live in the country

And I would always end the list by writing: *Thank you. Thank you. Thank you.*

Starting this was really challenging because let's face it: we're not in the habit of acknowledging the simple abundance already in our lives. Society is structured in such a way that we're always either thinking about what we don't have or looking at what someone else has instead of being grateful for the gifts in front of us.

Coming up with five items for your list might seem daunting at first, but with practice you'll grow in appreciation and have a stronger connection with the abundance already present in your life. Since I started the exercise of being grateful for everything, I have attracted an even more beautiful home and I am in deep appreciation for the simple things in everyday life. I appreciate watching birds go about their rituals, amazed at how perfect nature is. I believe that I am the healthiest I've ever been and it shows on the outside. It's not only my physical body that I appreciate now; it's everything and everyone around me. It appears that the more grateful I am, the more there is to be grateful for.

I should also mention that even life's challenges are reasons to be grateful because everything in life is an opportunity for learning even if it doesn't feel that way at the time. This is another habit that requires practice and is really worth the effort.

When something happens to shake up our life of course we feel overwhelmed and stressed. If you choose to develop a habit of gratitude, in time you will have the wisdom to press "refresh" and shift your response when the unthinkable happens.

By asking, "What can I learn from this situation?" there will always be an answer. We are certainly not in charge of life's events, however we are in charge of our response to them.

When we acknowledge that we can learn something from a challenging situation, we intentionally shift our energy from the freak-out place, which is a low vibration or negative energy, to a higher vibration or a positive energy. The shift creates awareness so we can use the power of the situation to learn! Don't forget that the law of attraction will match our vibration and bring us a situation that matches the energy or vibration that we're producing.

Lost in Transition

Here's an example from my adventures. As my husband and I were making our way to our time-share in Florida, we had a flight connection at Washington Dulles airport. When we landed, we found out that our connecting flight was oversold. We were bumped to another airline for a flight early the next day and sent to a hotel for a few hours' sleep. Somewhere between the bump and the hotel, my purse disappeared. Gasp!

It was one of those small swing bags I wore over my body, so trying to figure out where I might have left it was a puzzler. I was sure that I had not put it down anywhere. My entire being went into overdrive as my husband and I searched every square millimetre of the hotel room several times in disbelief. The bag that was missing held not only my cash but my passport, driver's license and credit card. I suddenly didn't exist and in these times of tight airport security, I was pretty sure that I had screwed up our holiday.

In the height of the drama, I called two of our friends who fortunately worked at the Canadian Embassy in Washington. They would help us get some sort of identification on Monday. So we spent the weekend in the Washington area and made the best of the situation. We also had to tack on a night in Washington at the end of our trip to get another document that would get me back into Canada. Talk about nerve wracking!

Okay, so here's where the road divides. I could have wallowed in that mess and lived off the story for months and at one time I might have done that. Instead, we regrouped after the initial rush of adrenaline, reminded ourselves of how fortunate we were to know somebody at the embassy, to be in a free country and to be warm and dry. I started there and although our vacation was more stressful than it should have been, I learned a number of valuable lessons.

The first lesson is that people in general are amazing and generous. Every person we talked to about what happened extended compassion and kindness. Our friends in Washington went above and beyond to make sure that we were comfortable and taken care of. The person who ended up with the contents of my purse may have needed them more than I do. I'll never know what really happened; I knew that I had to let that go too.

It took a while. I travelled through anger and self-pity to gratitude and now joy. I know how precious my passport is and I know that I have an incredible husband and fantastic friends (thank you, Kathy, Ian and Andre). I also learned to photocopy documentation and credit cards and carry them separately. I have a case for my passport that I wear under my clothes. I always thought people who wore those passport holders looked a little dorky, now I know they're very wise. I am grateful for every one of those lessons.

Had my identification not gone missing, I would not have been mindful to appreciate how great it is to live in a free country, where a passport can take us anywhere. I love my passport now and really value it. Before I lost it, my passport was a necessary inconvenience that had very little meaning to me. The stress of the situation – from not knowing if I would be able to travel to our destination to worrying if someone was using my identity in a sinister way – put a strain on every day of our time away together.

Although nothing ever came back from the unfortunate experience in Washington, I should mention that within two weeks of coming home, I had replaced all of my documentation. I truly hope that if anyone else finds themselves in a similar situation, they too will realize the gifts and the lessons in the experience.

Receiving is 'Giving'

What is your first response when someone tells you that you look great? Do you feel self-conscious and uncomfortable? Do you say "really?" or do you say thank you? The correct answer is of course to say thank you. If we acknowledge that this is all about energy and attracting what we want then it follows that by turning down a compliment we are saying, "No, I don't want that energy" and seriously, who doesn't love a compliment?

By accepting the energy in the compliment and saying thank you, we are opening the channel of good stuff coming our way. It follows too that if you make an effort to notice what is good and give compliments to others, you're signaling to the law of attraction that you have lots of good things to give away and so the law of attraction will match it to bring you more good things to give away.

You may think this idea is a little out there, so the only way to show you is to have you try it. For one day, notice something good about other people and let them know. It could be how they look; it could be about their work or their cooking. Make yourself available to receive the same type of energy from others and just observe how you feel at the end of the day. By the way, you should also curb any inclination to talk smack or be unkind because the law of attraction works to bring that energy back to you. Be open to receiving and see how you like it.

Meet my friend Kevin. He's a caring husband, son and father, as well as a thoughtful friend and a talented hair stylist. Kevin has a very attractive energy about him. Along with being very engaging and candid with his clients, he's also meticulous in his work. He's funny, generous, spiritual and wise. All of his clients love him and look forward to their visits in the salon.

At Christmas you can imagine that Kevin receives a lot of thoughtful gifts. One year, after achieving a weight loss goal, one of his regular clients gave him a pair of designer jeans. I happened to be seated next to this client while Kevin was having a conversation with her. He was clearly uncomfortable with her generosity and having explained that the jeans didn't fit him, he wanted her to take them back.

In their conversation, which I couldn't help but overhear, he kept refusing her offer and she kept trying to convince him that he would feel fantastic if he got the right pair of jeans. She wanted him to go with her to the store to make sure he was satisfied.

I couldn't get the conversation out of my mind and after giving it considerable thought, I called Kevin a few days later. What I realized was that he was actually turning away what he really wanted. He wanted to receive love and abundance, I know this from the many conversations we've had about the law of attraction. Keeping the law of attraction in mind and, as superficial as this example may appear, it's a perfect illustration of how we give out the message that we are not available to receive what we say we want.

If Kevin had graciously accepted the gift (making sure to use the magic words thank you) his client would have been overjoyed and he would have had a pair of designer jeans to show off his new body. But it's not really about jeans at all; it's about energy.

Remember that money is neither good nor bad, it is just energy. We assign the meaning to whether we have too much or not enough of that energy. We attract to us that which we focus on: either the lack or abundance through our thinking and our feelings.

In Kevin's case, if he interpreted the jeans as a gift of love (which is something he wants to receive), he could take the perceived monetary value of the gift and pay it forward by giving some of that energy to someone else. He could volunteer to cut hair for someone who couldn't afford it, he could do volunteer work or whatever he chose. As long as we keep the flow of energy going and feel grateful to receive what we really want, the Universe will recognize that we are available to receive it and will continue to match our request.

By shutting other people down when they give us a compliment or a gift, we are sending the message that we are not available and that it's not what we want. We may state very clearly what we want and then follow up with feelings of not being worthy or being overwhelmed with guilt about accepting. All the law of attraction recognizes is our feeling of unworthiness and guilt and not the very thing we are asking for.

Asking for what it is you want can be a little tricky and it takes practice. You need to be clear about it and then release all thought about the outcome. As hard as it is, we need to forget about feeding any negativity to the thought. Nurture yourself with goodness in your thinking and your feelings and you will have a healthy outcome.

In Kevin's case, he eventually decided to accept his client's generous gift. He didn't get designer jeans, but instead chose a beautiful new jacket that he loves.

Saying thank you and really meaning it will take work for some of us who are used to turning away from compliments and generosity from others. Just think about what you really want to attract into your life and see if you're available to receive what you're asking for. Gratitude is a powerful tool to help you shift to receiving.

Inspired Assignment:

Be mindful of using the words thank you; feel the true feeling of the words and use them often! Practice saying thank you and really mean it.

Start developing a habit of gratitude by writing what you're grateful for on the blank pages at the end of this chapter. Write down five things you are grateful for every day. It doesn't matter what it is, just do it every day. I guarantee that you will find more and more to be grateful for as you become more available for the law of attraction to deliver! Focus on all areas of your life – your physical body, your home, your family, your work environment, your community, your city, your country.

This next exercise feels really good. Send an e-mail, make a phone call or write a note to someone you appreciate. It can be someone you know or someone you encounter in the grocery store, at the gas station or your favorite restaurant. It can be about your relationship or it can be about how that person makes a difference.

Tell them why you are grateful for them; don't be afraid to say what is in your heart. If you're not much of a writer, head to the store and pick out a card that says what you would like to say.

Using this power tool of gratitude sends a very clear signal to the law of attraction that you are available to receive. Learn to be grateful for everything in your life and you will experience the magic that is meant for you alone.

Developing a habit of appreciation directs our thinking to the present moment, so that we don't miss what's happening in the now.

When you centre on gratitude, the law of attraction can match what you're asking for and deliver more to be grateful for.

*When we focus on the positive, we attract positive energy to us.
It's the law of attraction: like attracts like!*

Coming up with five items for your list might seem daunting at first, but with practice you'll grow in appreciation and have a stronger connection with the abundance already present in your life.

Feed yourself goodness in your thinking and your feelings and you will have a healthy outcome.

Courage

Every year at the end of our season when I was working on the television show, my work partner, Joel, and I would change up the format. We would do something fun together, often focused on food or an adventure of some kind.

One year, I came up with the idea to go to an aerial park – a place where you walk a course through the trees. Let me explain how the experience works: first you drive for an hour to the middle of nowhere, you strap on a safety harness and a helmet and you climb many metres straight up a steep ladder attached to the side of a tree. You then clip your harness on to a safety cable and cross from one tree to another.

You might navigate your way across by stepping on skinny slats of wood that swing back and forth like trapezes; you might walk a balance beam or maybe crawl across on a ladder. When you reach the other side, you then unhook from the safety line and fasten your harness on to a skinny metal cable or zip line that stretches hundreds of metres, sometimes across a small lake. To accomplish this, you hang on to the cable for dear life with leather gloved hands and fling yourself off a platform.

The next thing you know, you're flying through the air like Peter Pan without the charming Disney effects. You slow the momentum you pick up by tightening your gloved hand on the cable; it's a soft landing with plenty of padding on the platform. Once there, you gather your courage and prepare for the next leg of the course.

We thought this experience would make excellent visuals, so in the interest of making great television our small team went to the aerial park for a day of "play." The folks at the park were really helpful. They took us to a practice course and showed us the ropes, so to speak. On the practice course, the zip lines were about a metre off the ground and the other challenges were low too, so I kept asking myself: why are we even wearing helmets?

As I explained, we wanted to give our viewers the best experience of the park, so our guide took us right to the final and most challenging section of the course. When we got to our starting point, I was doing my best to appear composed. Now my thinking mind was having a fear field day. "Who am I kidding? How am I going to get this done?"

There was the added pressure that two cameras were with us: one on the ground and one up in the trees with Joel and me. We started our ascent toward the sky, straight up the side of a towering tree. The whole time I was climbing I was thinking that this had to be one of the craziest things I'd ever done. There was a little fear of heights mixed in with fear of trying something new up in the trees all while the television cameras filmed our every move. As a result, I was a bit of a mess! Joel was brave and encouraging as he crossed from tree to tree, making it look easy and reassuring me through each challenge.

I had an epiphany when I crossed a particularly difficult section of the course. It was the part that had wooden trapezes set just far enough apart that it was close to impossible for a vertically challenged person like me to navigate. As soon as I stepped on to the platform, Joel said "Look at you, you left your fear on the other side."

That moment was one I'll never forget. It was in that instant, in a flash really, I realized that anything is possible. If I could climb up the side of a tree despite my fear, if I could make my way through this challenging course despite fear, imagine what else I could do in the face of fear. I don't even want to call it "my" fear anymore because I do not want to own fear, I want to manage it. Many zip lines and life challenges later, I now have the courage to set aside what other people think and actually write this book. How is that for courage?

Using courage is a way to shine light into the darkness of fear, to illuminate the path to confidence and success. It is a power tool, fired by your belief in whatever your dream may be. That particular day, my fear was centered on surviving the aerial adventure in the trees and my vision was to provide a fun experience for our viewers to enjoy. I got way more out of the escapade than I ever expected. Perhaps that's a lesson we can learn from fear. It's there to protect us from harm, so if we're safe, even if it's scary, why not push through with courage? You might just leave your fear on the other side, like I did.

Fear Factor

North Americans suffered like never before in the first decade of the new millennium. Intense fear reigned after the events of September 11, 2001 when the World Trade Center towers were destroyed by suicide bombers. We all lost something in that horrific attack, whether it was a loved one, our sense of security or our innocence. It took great courage to get up the next day and go forward, even if we didn't know anybody who was directly affected.

Since that time, North America has been on a downhill slide. Fear seems to be all around us and many people do whatever they can to run from it. Fear of job loss or financial ruin, fear of aging, fear of not having enough, fear of looking at who we truly are. We have come up with habits to calm our fear that ultimately do nothing to manage it. Our self-medicating practices simply shift our focus temporarily and some of them are killing us. We use food, alcohol, drugs, sex, gossip and shopping as coping tools to keep fear at bay, rather than managing it by speaking directly to it. The only way fear will sit down is if it's asked to do so and the only way we ask it to sit down is by telling it what we want.

Mining to discover what we really want means examining what is our heart's desire. It's a feeling of want without the feeling of lack attached to it. What do you want really means what do you desire?

As I began this journey of *Inspiration in Action*, I didn't know what I wanted. My husband uses a great coaching expression: "If you don't know where you're going, any road will get you there." Frankly it's draining to not know what you want; by contrast, it's motivating to know what you do want.

Inspired Assignment:

Let's look at an exercise in courage that you can begin right now and come back to it as your ideas begin to marinate. On the blank pages that follow, write the heading WHAT I DON'T WANT across the top of the page and list below everything that you don't want. For example: I don't want to feel lonely. I don't want to have to cook dinner every night. I don't want to be broke.

It doesn't matter what's on your list, just get it on paper, so you can see clearly what it is you don't want in your life. This is a very courageous step. You might start the list today and come back to it another time to add more. Just start somewhere because when you do, you magically begin to shift the energy of your thinking, which gives the law of attraction something different and eventually more positive to work with.

Remember that the law of attraction doesn't decipher between do and don't; all it hears is what you want. So if we say for example "I don't want to be broke," we're focusing on what we don't want and asking the law of attraction to bring that. We need to shift the language we use with ourselves to begin the journey of changing the outcome. A clearer message about what we want in this example would be to say "I want abundance or I want to feel abundant." Once you have a list of what you don't want, you're in a perfect position to start being clear with yourself about what you do want.

Saying that you don't want to be broke really doesn't offer much to work with, don't you agree? It's a general statement that has no substance while containing a lot of feeling. Use the power tool of gratitude to help shift the energy from feeling broke to feeling abundant. I strongly suggest using pen and paper to list the abundance you already have, starting with your breath.

Once you shift your focus to gratitude for what you already have, you're signaling to the law of attraction, to that universal divine energy, to bring you more abundance. There you have it – you've shifted from a "lack" mindset, in this case, feeling broke, to an abundant mindset. Then practice, practice, practice and shift out of lack when the old habit pops up.

Continue the exercise for each item on your list of what you don't want and find inside of you how to turn the statement into what you do want. If you get stuck, try sharing the challenge with someone, whether it's a friend or a professional. Then on another blank page write WHAT I DO WANT and list what you want having done the exercise above. You might be surprised to discover the gifts hidden among the limited beliefs you hold about your life. Shift your thoughts and your feelings to make yourself more available to receive.

Of course, once you know what it is you do want, the responsibility then becomes keeping your thoughts, feelings and actions in line with what you want, again signaling to the law of attraction that this is what you are available to receive. Fuel this new direction with gentle reminders to yourself to focus on what you want. Be patient and tender with yourself and take it one thought at a time.

Moving On

While our economic picture slowly improves, many people are in need of support to go forward. It was announced during the 2010 Olympics in Vancouver, British Columbia that ABC News in the U.S. had laid off 25% of their staff. It was a warning for the rest of us working in the industry. The business of television has been forced to operate in a different way since the Internet began slowly eroding viewership. The markets have been shifting as more people rely on their computers for news and entertainment. Those of us working in the business held out hope that we would be able to keep our jobs in these uncertain times.

That same year, our chief anchor at the TV station – someone I thought of as my mentor – announced that he had decided to retire. We knew the day was coming, but when it happened many of us on staff felt that everything we thought we knew had changed. Our leader was gone and our future was uncertain.

When I got up the next day I was really down. I knew that I had to grieve the past and so I did. Luckily it was a Saturday so I stayed in my pajamas. I thought about the past and everything we had shared with our boss: one of our colleagues had been murdered on the property after his sportscast and another colleague died from a heart attack. We also lost our newsroom in a fire about two months prior to the boss's retirement.

I had to examine how I wanted to go forward and I realized that I needed to call upon courage to help. It took some soul searching and at the end of that Saturday I promised myself that I would not buy into the fear that was surely going to be the predominant mood. I acknowledged that I was not in charge of the situation. It wasn't my company and so whatever was going to happen was going to happen whether I lost sleep or I slept like a baby; whether I worried about it or I applied that energy to doing the best job I could. I made a promise to bring my thinking back to the moment when the fear crept in.

I worked hard to give myself small gifts: yoga, meditation, hot baths, quiet time, a manicure, pedicure, any kind of self-care that would make me feel good. When I call on courage, even when I say the word, I feel empowered. I knew that I would survive whatever lay ahead and deal with it when it showed up.

Over the next two years, I used a lot of courage to navigate through uncertainty at the television station. Then our new general manager announced that the company would be changing its business model and severance packages were available to anyone on staff who didn't want to go through the changes. My dream was to leave the station within two years, once my book was finished, to teach seminars and to follow my vision of helping other people discover their own magnificence. So I found the courage to say yes to the silver handshake (it wasn't quite golden) and left to start the next chapter of this incredible adventure.

I think my boss was a little surprised that I had found the courage to thank him for giving me the opportunity to move on. I wanted to do that to signal to the law of attraction that there was only good stuff going on here. I knew that I needed to leave everything in a really good light because everything looks better with good lighting. Courage has helped me to navigate the transition from full-time work to full-time passion.

Good Vibrations

A few years ago, while on vacation in Cozumel with my wonderful husband, we joined a table of guests on our first night at the resort. There were seven of us and the conversation was lively. Two of the women were teachers as was my mother and my husband's father so we had some great discussions about the state of the classroom today.

One of the couples was from New York State – let's call them Jim and Kelly – they were celebrating their 24th wedding anniversary. They mentioned that one of their children was living in New York City and they were so proud of his accomplishments.

We asked how many children they had and Jim said that they had three, but one had died. We all offered our sympathy and then Kelly explained that their son was five when he was killed in a car crash. She added that she was never sure what to say when people asked about their family. Sometimes she said that they had two children and sometimes she said three.

It had been many years since their son had passed away and they still both had trouble talking about it. Kelly and Jim wanted their son's life to have meaning and could not believe that there is a reason for everything. How could this young life ending so early make sense to anybody? I could feel the hurt in Kelly's voice as she shared just the tiniest bit of her private pain.

I never saw Kelly and Jim again, but I sent them a lot of compassion and hope that they would be able find the courage to flip their thinking about their son. In their grief, they had been focusing on what they didn't have and so the law of attraction brought them more grief. If they were able to begin to focus on the blessings that their child brought to their lives and celebrate him in some way, the law of attraction would bring peace and their son's spirit would be with them forever in the most beautiful way.

Grief is a challenging and unique experience. I certainly can't tell anybody else how to feel around the loss of their loved one. What I do know is that at some point we need to live. We carry the memories and the beauty of each person we have known in our hearts and can honor them by keeping their spirit alive and inspiring other people. It takes courage to change the direction of our thinking when we are in pain. When we ask courage to support us in nurturing a new perspective about our situation, we will see a different result. The law of attraction will make sure of that!

Remember that all emotion is energy and all energy is vibration. On the scale of vibrations that emotions emit, shame being the lowest vibration and joy or love being the highest, courage is in the middle, right below willingness. While a situation may appear difficult, even impossible, we can call upon courage and ask for the support we need to go ahead and face whatever perceived block might be holding us back. Courage will always help us to move through fear. Walk with courage when you are afraid and experience the miracle. Your vibration will shift and the law of attraction will do what it has to do to match your vibration. Stay in the fear and the Universe will match that too.

When we use courage to begin to change our mind, we immediately move to willingness and start the journey toward joy. This shift makes room for a new more purposeful practice that will take us where we really want to go.

Rachel's Rock Star Moment

Meet Rachel, one of the original members of *Inspiration in Action*, who at the age of 35 has insight far beyond her chronological age. She shares a great story about how she used courage to push past fear.

"To some people singing karaoke might be no big deal, but for me it was really scary. One night I was out with a group of pals at a karaoke bar and my friend Tammy said, 'Go up there and sing a song, Rachel.' I told her that there was nothing she could say to me that would make me sing a karaoke song . . . nothing, so stop trying.

Then I pictured myself going up and singing and I could feel my heart racing. I started to shake, my hands went cold and there was just this all-encompassing fear. I was talking to myself and there was all this action going on around me in the bar and I thought to myself, 'What's going on here? What is it really? What am I afraid of? I'm afraid people are going to judge me.'

But then I thought, 'What's the worst thing that could happen here? The worst thing is that I die, right? That's really the worst thing possible. Am I going to die? No! It was really one of those moments where I had to go and do it because I had a fear of it.'

So I went up on stage and sang. It probably wasn't very good, but it didn't matter. It was just that I did it! I sang 'Sunday Bloody Sunday' by U2, which is a lot harder than I thought it was. When I'm in the car singing with them, it doesn't seem that hard. Anyway, it was actually fun and now I know that although it was challenging to get there, it's one more thing that I know I am capable of doing. I've done it, I could do it again and there are so many situations where I can apply courage in the future to help me push past my fear. I really don't want to take a back seat in my life. I want to be right out there living my life."

Rachel's example shows that our thinking mind will have us believe that we're quite comfortable, thank you very much, without taking any risks. Why put yourself out there to be judged? If we don't take risks, we can never know what's possible. Even at the risk of being judged, why not try something that scares you just a little. As long as you're safe, you really have nothing to lose and so much wisdom to gain. While Rachel doesn't make her living singing karaoke, she has the courage to try it any time. In fact, she and a few other friends encouraged me to sing with them at my birthday party a few years ago. It's something I wouldn't have had the courage to do on my own and you know what? It was really fun!

Running Full On

Meet Ray Zahab, an endurance runner who lives close to my home. By the time we met, he had become an international running star, raising awareness for important causes with every step he took. All I knew about Ray was that he was the guy who ran on the side of the road, pulling a tire attached by a rope to his waist. Seriously, he still does it to train his body to pull weight.

When I had the opportunity to do a story on Ray for our TV show, I learned about his successes and I learned about his story of surrender. Ray is known all over the world as an ultra-marathon runner and someone who makes a difference through his foundation called I2P, which stands for Impossible to Possible. He is committed to inspiring young people to make a difference by sharing his amazing expeditions with them. Students follow his travels from their classroom; he's also arranged to have some of them carry out their own supervised expeditions, proving that they can do anything. Ray knows firsthand how to make the impossible possible; he's done it many times!

Ray grew up on a horse farm just outside of Ottawa, Ontario where he learned to train horses. In his 20s, Ray was a party animal, a smoker and a self-described couch potato. He was lost and even though that wasn't how other people saw him, it was the message he was sending out to the law of attraction. There was no passion, no connection with anything meaningful until Ray chose to take a closer look at what was really going on and the shift began.

He told me that at one point he looked around at the people in his life who were getting results and was inspired by his younger brother, John, a successful personal trainer who was happy in his life. Ray made the conscious choice to take the road his brother had taken to see if he could change the results in his own life. He soon became a personal trainer with an online coaching business.

By going mountain biking with his brother, being active and staying positive in his thinking and in his life, Ray was opening opportunities to discover what else was out there for him. One day he picked up a magazine about endurance running and saw photographs of people who looked like him as opposed to his perceived idea of what endurance runners should look like.

He wondered what would happen if he tried endurance running and after three months of training, Ray found himself at the start of a race in Canada's far north. He would be running through snow, a sled with all of his gear on board (that's where pulling the tire training fits in). About half way through the race, Ray wanted to stop and go home. He thought that this was the wildest idea he had ever followed up on. Then he remembered a promise he made to himself to do his best and never look back. One foot in front of the other, he continued and the kilometres blew by. Ray not only finished that race, he won it.

Since then there have been many courageous expeditions on ice and sand, to the South Pole, through the Gobi and Sahara Deserts, as well as the Amazon River. Each one has been an amazing journey!

In 2011, Ray joined two other world class runners, one from the United States, the other from Korea, to run the Sahara Desert. They planned to run through six countries, not only as a test of their abilities, but to raise awareness of the water shortage in these desert communities. Their project came to the attention of Oscar-winning film director James Moll, who told actor and producer Matt Damon about it. James directed and Matt was executive producer and narrator for the film, "*Running the Sahara*," which documents the experience shared by the three runners as they spent 111 incredible days in the desert. When they completed the run, all three put their hands in the Red Sea. Ray said to me after achieving this remarkable feat, "you know what was different about us? Nothing!"

The other two runners were in the top of their class and even though Ray had been running for only two years at that point, he knew then with certainty that with courage there were no limits on what he could accomplish. He continues to believe that there are no limits on what any of us can achieve.

Reach for the Sky

It takes courage to push past the thinking that keeps our dreams locked in our imagination. Each step we take will be met with reward and the knowing that we are in charge of our dreams. Getting them out into the world will be the best way to fully know our life's mission. It all starts with our thoughts and our feelings. Change them and you will change your life!
It could be singing karaoke or taking up exercise. It could be painting, doing stand-up comedy or dancing. It could be losing weight or trying new make-up or clothing. My friend Katherine, a documentary filmmaker and visual artist, says that she feels empowered each day, knowing that she can call on courage to assist her in doing anything. Just saying the word courage flips the energy of our vibration to an opening rather than being closed off by fear. I think of courage as my friend now, something I can call on for support when I'm afraid.

It's important to remember that fear keeps our light dim. By using courage like a power tool to up the wattage, we create a ripple effect that spills into all areas of our lives. When fear owns us we feel trapped and helpless; we are far away from who we truly are.

We are born magnificent beings and somehow over time, we forget. I say somehow and yet I know how. It's conditioning and limited beliefs. It's the messages that people like our parents give to us from their limited beliefs and we trust that they are correct. It's the drama in someone else's life or in our thinking mind and we believe it. We are none of it and it requires great courage to remember who we truly are. Those of us who believe in a power greater than ourselves understand that we're spiritual beings having a human experience. We ascribe positive attributes to the powerful force that created us; if we are part of that energy then we must have that energy in us. "You are not just a drop in the ocean. You are the mighty ocean in a drop," says 13th century Persian poet and Sufi mystic, Rumi.

I believe that it takes courage to acknowledge that we are not what our thinking mind would have us believe we are. Our thinking mind is limited and wants to keep us safe. As Marianne Williamson says, "Our greatest fear is not that we are inadequate, our greatest fear is that we are powerful beyond measure." That's the wisdom I hope you will connect with.

Some limited thinkers are certain that we are human beings period. They see no connection between their mind and their body and can't understand that what they think and how they think influences what happens in their body and in their life.

Limited thinkers are using the law of attraction too without knowing it. The law brings them more limiting experiences because that's what they're focusing their thoughts and feelings on. They don't realize that the body, mind and spirit are all one. There's no shame or blame in this matter and it's certainly not my mission to judge anybody for how they view their world. In fact, I am very careful about who I share myself with now because I know that many limited thinkers feel uncomfortable around this type of conversation.

I understand that what you think of me is none of my business, so I do my best to be inspiration in action: extending compassion and kindness to people who feel the need to judge. It takes courage to be present in the moment without judgment and greater courage to be love. I believe I will practice this for the rest of my life.

In his works, Eckhart Tolle talks about who we are as the vast blue sky and our thoughts as clouds coming and going. Sometimes the clouds are light and fluffy and sometimes they're dark and dense, but the light always shines through the clouds. We are the infinite sky – when I first heard that idea it took my breath away because it really gave me an image to refer to and a cue for me to remember who I truly am – I am the sky.

Call upon the power tool of courage to remind your thinking mind that you are powerful beyond measure. When we look at affirmations in another chapter, you can choose specific statements that resonate with you and help connect you with your true self. The habit of repeating affirmations is a power tool that asks fear to sit down by telling it what you want and who you are. For now, have courage to be with the idea that you are not who you think you are. You are not your thoughts, you are not your story (your past), you are not your friends, you are not your job. Taking your thinking mind or ego out of the equation, you are powerful beyond anything your thinking mind could conjure.

I also believe that it takes courage to share ourselves with others. Most of us have a long list of reasons why we keep our cards close to our chest; why we don't share ourselves. The reasons usually relate to past hurt and fear about what might happen if we open up to others. If we believe that we are not our thoughts, not our relationships, not our jobs and not our past then as we share ourselves with others, we signal to the law of attraction that we are available for some movement of energy, a new story, a new experience.

Then we can share ourselves from whatever we have, whether it is an abundance of smiles, time, kindness, money, cookies, errand running or whatever it is, and not expect anything in return. Our giving is unconditional and the law of attraction matches the good vibration or energy of our giving and provides more. Since there are no blockages, this completes the cycle of giving and receiving. This law of attraction works 24/7 and is ready to deliver the moment we have the courage to receive. There's an expression that goes something like, "Whatever it is you want, give it to someone else." *The Mindfulness Project*, which we'll look at a little later, is about sharing to complete the cycle of receiving and giving.

Inspired Assignment:

It takes courage to uncover what it is you want, so you send a clear signal to the law of attraction. This exercise will be helpful because it's often a real challenge to figure out what is our heart's desire or what we really want.

On the blank pages that follow, write the word COURAGE across one of the pages and below it list what you would love to do if you had the confidence to do it. Come on now, you only have one life to live, what's it going to be?

Getting these ideas out of your imagination and on to paper is a fantastic starting point and signals to the law of attraction that you are available to start giving form to these dreams. Then start talking about your dreams with people you trust and toss around some ideas about how you can start taking baby steps toward bringing them to life. This is exactly how *Inspiration in Action: A Woman's Guide to Happiness* evolved and is still evolving.

Use courage to share yourself with people you encounter. Smile and make eye contact with strangers, knowing that you are connected to them. Let's stop being so afraid of one another and extend a little more kindness. Think of ways in which you can share the unique gifts you have to offer. Be mindful about it, knowing that you could be changing someone's day with a small gesture.

It takes courage to change the direction of our thinking when we are in pain. When we ask courage to support us in nurturing a new perspective about our situation, we will see a different result.

Courage will always help us to move through fear.

*When we use courage to begin to change our mind,
we immediately move to willingness and start the
journey toward joy.*

Remember that the law of attraction doesn't decipher between do and don't; all it hears is what you want.

Just saying the word courage flips the energy of our vibration to an opening rather than being closed off by fear.

If we don't take risks, we can never know what's possible.

Surrender and Release

The self-storage business in North America nets over $30 billion a year. Most of us have stuff stashed in cupboards, basements, garages and storage lockers. I am by no means a minimalist – I love beautiful things. Thankfully, our home has minimal storage space, so we have to be mindful about not holding on to too much and we still have way more stuff than we need!

Getting that first apartment and buying furniture is usually where collecting stuff begins. We acquire, inherit, borrow and purchase stuff for the rest of our lives. We cherish certain items for sentimental, investment or aesthetic reasons and we hold on to things that have no meaning whatsoever, usually because we think we can't part with them. Eventually we end up with more stuff than we have room for and there's always more waiting in the stores for us to bring home, when we tire of the stuff we have.

I try to live by this clutter clearing rule: if I want something new, I have to move something out to create space to receive what I want. I try to be mindful that it's the cycle of giving and receiving. I get really excited when I know that I am going to share some stuff with friends or move some things to the consignment store or to a deserving charity.

I see it as an opportunity to share abundance. I recently went through my costume jewelry and put what I don't absolutely love and what I don't wear into a pretty box. I shared it with my girlfriends and with a women's shelter. It felt good to surrender that "stuff" and it made room for me to attract more of what I love. Not long after surrendering the jewelry, I received two beautiful necklaces for my birthday. I love them both; I'll do it again when the time comes so I can share whatever it is I don't need or use with someone who will appreciate it.

My dear friend Suzanne did the same thing when she came to stay with us for a few days. She packed her suitcase with some beautiful purses she didn't need any more. I fell in love with them and was so grateful for her thoughtfulness. When the new bags arrived, I wanted to give up some of what I already had. The next time I got together with a group of girlfriends, I put the purses I needed to move out of my closet in the back of my car and invited the girls to "shop." It was a delightful moment and a beautiful example of giving and receiving.

My sister-in-law is a talented decorator and personal stylist who taught me that if I bring an item of clothing into my closet, I have to let one item go. I do try to honor that practice because it minimizes clutter. While this is something I am constantly working on, I know that when I share what I don't need with someone who needs it more than I do, I am actually making myself more attractive to receive what I want. I am in effect creating space in my life to receive. These examples are really superficial, but they point to the fact that we all have stuff and holding on to it keeps us stuck.

Clear the Clutter

Surrendering happens on many levels in our lives and it's something most of us humans are reluctant to take part in. We're comfortable with our stuff, right? The stuff in our closets and drawers, in the basement, garage or off-site storage is taking up valuable real estate in our mind. The aim of *Inspiration in*

Action is to clear the clutter and make ourselves available to receive what it is we really want.

We do inventory when we want to de-clutter our stuff; I want to encourage you to do the same with what goes on in your thinking mind. Choose what YOU want to hold on to: the thoughts, feelings, situations and people that support you in achieving what you want to accomplish with your life and what really is your heart's desire.

When we hold on to stuff from our past, whether it is old programming or other people's drama, we are allowing those false ideas or illusions to run the show and really dictate how our life will unfold. Remember that it's called the past for a reason; all we know for sure is this present moment.

Carrying around the baggage of the past is not only a heavy burden; it also acts as a barrier, preventing us from accessing our dreams. Surrendering the stories and the clutter in our thinking mind instantly shifts energy and creates an opening for us to receive.

Remember that what we resist persists, so hold on to your stuff if it's giving you the results you want and if not, it's time to take stock. Whatever activity is going on in our thinking mind is informing our future. The law of attraction works with our thoughts and feelings, bringing to us whatever it is we're asking for with them.

For years, I had the running story that my mother's disapproval held me back from living the life I wanted. I had a curiosity about the world that my mother was afraid of; I was a challenge for her every step of the way. I'm sure at times she thought the hospital gave her the wrong baby!

Where I wanted freedom and permission to chase my dreams, my mother was overprotective, critical and discouraging. Her fear instilled doubt that I would be able to realize my goals. She wanted me to shoot low and I wanted to go for the stars.

My Mum wasn't comfortable supporting me in my pursuit of a career in broadcasting. She wanted me to learn typing and shorthand to pursue what she thought was a stable occupation. I just couldn't imagine the results that my mother wanted me to achieve – all I could see in my imagination were my dreams.

I felt sure that I was meant to be a broadcaster, which she thought was an unstable profession. My father worked in public relations, dealing with media professionally and partying with them in the course of doing business. Alcohol consumption was part of the arrangement and I think that my mother was afraid for me because my father was an alcoholic, as were many of his chums. Of course, I didn't realize what her concerns were about at the time. She was expressing love and all I heard was no, no, no.

Looking back now, it certainly was an interesting ride. I learned along the way that people show their love in peculiar ways and I learned a lot about being independent. The biggest lesson for me was learning to believe in the power of my dreams. Eventually, I learned not to fill my head with my mother's beliefs. How my mother saw what I wanted and what I wanted were totally different. My passion trumped her desire and I found my way through the maze to cultivate a successful broadcasting career. I was able to clear the clutter so that I could hear my own truth.

Life Lessons

Frannie (my nickname for my mother, Fran) had challenges of her own growing up. Her father was against her dream of pursuing a career as a teacher. He wanted her to give up on education, settle down and start a family. Despite her father's insistence, my mother did both by becoming a popular grade school teacher and having a family. My parents moved us from coast to coast when my father was transferred with CP Rail. Frannie ran our household almost singlehandedly. It wasn't until she was in her 50s that she pursued a university degree. Looking back, I have great admiration for her. I can't imagine how she did it all.

My mother was one of my best teachers, but I saw her as my adversary while I was growing up. I just couldn't get comfortable in my relationship with her. We seemed to be at opposite ends. She was a fearful person who rarely let her feelings show and I wore my heart on my sleeve. As challenging as it was and as much as the little girl in me craved acceptance, I knew that if I wanted to move ahead in my life, I had to learn to let go of the need for my mother's approval. I began to discover that it was my responsibility to do what was right for me. Man, that was frightening!

I wanted to become a broadcaster, to connect with and somehow comfort people through communication. I didn't fully understand this dream; I just knew I had to follow the path. On one hand, I was sure I knew what I wanted, but I was also afraid of being seen for who I really am: a sensitive, caring person. I had received the message that the way I felt was not acceptable. I was sure that my mother's criticism of my lifestyle combined with my inability to live up to her dream for me, was preventing me from achieving what I wanted. I was a disappointment. I was sure of it.

I felt uneasy and unsure around my parents and around most people for that matter. I felt powerless in my own life and yet I continued to chase my dream. I couldn't see two feet in front of me, I just did exactly as the teachers of law of attraction tell us: I held a visual image of doing what I dreamt of in my imagination and for some unexplainable reason I just believed it.

Over time I began to clear the clutter in my thinking mind by surrendering the poor messaging I received in the relationships I had with my parents. I also encouraged myself to nurture a better rapport with my dreams. I started to work on loving my mother for who she was. It took a few years of therapy to kick start the process and since then I have practiced forgiveness and compassion: first for myself, then for my Mum. Frannie's stuff was her stuff and my stuff is my stuff!

If I had continued in the clutter, I would not have seen that my parents did the best job they could and I wouldn't have known the power of courage to help me unplug from the need to have their approval. When I shifted my thinking, my feelings shifted over time as well and the direction of my life became clearer. I began to experience a difference in the response I was getting from people around me and in the people being drawn into my life. There was a lot more love coming through. Love is one of the big ticket items on the list of what I want, so I'm pleased that I'm more available to receive it now.

My mother died in her late 80s and by then I had known the pleasure of a relationship with her without much anxiety because I simply did not engage. I believed in who I was more than I believed what she thought about me. What a blessing, what a miracle!

Freedom Begins with a Single Thought

Perhaps for you it's a message you received from someone in your life, a misunderstanding from your childhood or maybe you simply thought life would go one way and it went another. Whether it's what we call low self-esteem, a lack of worthiness or feeling lost, the messages that got us there play over and over in our thinking mind, keeping us stuck.

I believe it was Einstein who said, "we can't solve problems by using the same kind of thinking we used when we created them." We need to surrender and release the messages that aren't in line with our goals and dreams by focusing on thoughts that will bring us what we want. If your reaction to my proposal is to say "Well, she has absolutely no idea how hurt I was by . . . or she doesn't know me and my situation, I was violated by so and so in such a way that I just can't let it go." It could be that you feel you have wounded someone and your thinking mind has you stuck in the mindset that feeling badly somehow helps. It's like poisoning yourself. Seriously, it is.

It does not help you and it certainly does nothing for whomever you're feeling so badly about. By releasing yourself from the repeated messaging in your thinking mind, you will focus on gratitude for the blessings in your life and begin to shift the focus of your thoughts. In time those thoughts will no longer run your show. It takes great courage to stand in the truth and the truth is that none of those stories define you in this moment. The present moment is all we know for sure and in this moment you and I are absolutely perfect exactly as we are. The stories that spin in your thinking mind are not true in this moment. Period. The challenge for us is to be present, accepting that life is as it is now without the stories.

These days, I find myself having to surrender any attachment to how other people view me and my life adventures. I mentioned earlier that I left my television job after 24 years to set out on this fantastic creative pursuit. Sometimes when I tell people about the book, especially when I tell them the title of it, their eyes get very wide. I never really know what they're thinking.

I used to feel self-conscious because I felt that people would judge my choice, but now I'm settling into the idea of living as a life artist and now I love to explain what that means to people who ask. I tell them that we all create our lives with our thoughts and I want my life to be joyful, fun, abundant, prosperous, peaceful, beautiful and loving, so I think thoughts that are aligned with what I want. I realize now that it's my responsibility to be *Inspiration in Action*.

Surrendering to Receive

The day I decided to surrender my anxiety around money, I received a cheque in the mail for $1,000. It was a completely unexpected gift from a special person in my life. Earlier that day, I had been listening to an interview with Hale Dwoskin, the author of *The Sedona Method*, as I drove around, running errands. He was explaining how the method worked, much as they describe in *The Secret*. We are our own worst enemies when it comes to attracting what we want. We have barriers in our mind that prevent us from allowing what we want to show up in our lives.

I was completely on board with Hale's theory. I listened eagerly as he walked us through how his plan works. He asked us to be present with a situation that had been causing some problem, whether it was around relationships or money, whatever it was, to be as present as we could be with the feeling. I reached in and pulled up the anxiety I have always had when the topic of money would come up. Then he asked if we could live without that feeling and my answer was ABSOLUTELY YES!

Next he asked when we would be willing to give up that feeling and my answer was NOW! I wanted freedom from that anxiety; I want to be comfortable with money and of course, I want to use the law of attraction to bring baskets of it into my life. So in that moment, I surrendered my fear and did a little happy dance in my seat as I drove around town.

I picked up the mail on my way home and because my birthday had been the previous day, I was tickled to see a few birthday cards in the mailbox. What I did not expect was the cheque for $1,000 that was enclosed in one of the birthday cards. You could have knocked me over with a feather. The next day in the mail, there was another unexpected cheque for $22. I had begun a process of relinquishing the anxiety I had around money and the Universe was bringing into form that which I desired.

Admittedly, I am on a journey that is sometimes bumpy and even blocked. When I feel fear emerge, I consciously shift the thought and the emotion to feeling good and recognizing the abundance in my life. I use the power tool of gratitude to let go of the negative vibration and shift it to a positive feeling.

"I have enough" and "I am enough" are two of the affirmations I use to replace the negative feeling of lack (more on affirmations a little later). I recognize now that it was the feeling of lack that I was projecting that kept what I wanted from coming into my life.

While my old behavior is still around, I recognize it when it shows up and I work to consciously shift my thinking and feelings so that there's more of the abundance than there is lack in my mind. I work at it every day, sometimes successfully and sometimes my storyteller wins, however I keep working because abundance is another one of the big ticket items on the list of what I want.

Train your Thoughts

The object of the exercise is to be IN THE PROCESS, so that gradually more and more of what you want will appear and less and less you'll return to feelings of what you don't want. It is magic! If you give yourself permission and allow your mind to be open, you'll learn that creating a happier, more peaceful life is easier than your storyteller or left brain thinking allows you to believe.

The great news is that we're in charge of it all. I know that sometimes we feel like we're not in charge of much in the world but we do choose our thoughts. Once I started to see the results of surrendering the thoughts that don't serve my goals, I could see my dreams more clearly in my imagination. If my thinking mind gets too active, sometimes I imagine a beautiful waterfall to take my thoughts off of whatever story is running. I see all kinds of gorgeous plants and birds in my mind; I hear the sound of the water and feel the feeling of being in that place. It's a soothing gift to my thinking mind; a break from all of the work it does.

There are so many fantastic benefits to choosing your thoughts wisely. At one time, I resented receiving bills, but now I pay them gratefully. I appreciate having a telephone that connects me with family, friends and business opportunities, so I joyfully take care of the bill in appreciation for that service. It can be challenging when money is tight, however what I want is abundance so I am working on focusing on abundance in order to attract what I desire.

Our power is not tied to our status, stature or style! Real power lives in the knowing that our past is not in any way controlling our lives; our power is in the present moment. When we listen to the subtle voice of the soul and acknowledge the pure, beautiful, abundant and endless supply of courage and inspiration available, why wouldn't we want to surrender the story that is holding us back? When we keep looking back, going over and over our perceived mistakes, we stay stuck in that past. When we project into the future, we are not available for what's happening in the present. The present is perfect; what is done is done. All we have to do is learn from the past and do better in the present.

We are conditioned to have all the answers and not to sit with the questions. Is it such a bad thing not to always have the answer when someone asks you what you're going to do now that you've lost your job, your home or your partner? In each case the solutions take time and investigation, often first within ourselves. We need to extend kindness to ourselves first and resist caring what other people think of our process. Look for people in your circle who understand that trauma takes time to work through and lean on them. Surrender and release, the next step will show itself!

Not all of us are comfortable sharing our "stuff" in conversation with family, friends or even counselors. I encourage you to investigate how you can surrender your stuff and begin the shift to empowering your pure and perfect self, opening your heart to receiving what you really want.

I think that next to learning to be grateful for what we have, surrendering what we don't want is an important step in becoming attractive to receiving, so that the Universe can help us to realize our dreams.

Back to School

You've heard the saying, "When the student is ready; the teacher appears." Our teachers often show up in positions of some power in our lives: parents, siblings, close friends and bosses. I think they're in those positions so we'll be sure to notice them. Some of our teachers are kind and nurturing and some are critical and controlling. We often don't realize the benefit of the lessons we learn from our teachers until we look back and appreciate that those people were in our path for a purpose, even if it wasn't pleasant at the time.

As I said earlier, I am one of many women who had a tumultuous relationship with her mother. We knew how to push each other's buttons and it wasn't until my mother was rather elderly that I learned the most precious lesson from our relationship. I was in the habit of letting Frannie's negativity and criticism run my storyteller. I developed that habit early in life and cultivated quite a poor self-image over the years as a result. The rules in our relationship changed dramatically when I understood that if there was no audience, there was no show. If I didn't engage in her negativity, she wouldn't get the response she was looking for and it pretty much resolved my problem. What I received was a taste of the peace I was searching for in my heart.

I have had a few bosses who taught me tough lessons too and I love them now because I see more clearly looking back that their role in my life was to teach, not to drive me crazy, which was what I thought at the time.

We attract exactly what we need to teach us in every moment. When we're not ready to notice the opportunity a situation presents, we'll continue in the same place until we choose to learn and grow from the experience.

We are the product of our choices and when we stay in the past, allowing our storyteller to have the power, our thoughts, feelings and vibrations are dictated by that state. The instant we relinquish the story, the vibration begins to shift because our feelings alter and the law of attraction matches our new vibration, bringing new situations and new people to answer our request. It's like putting in an order at the take-out window: what you ask for is what you receive.

This life experience is an amazing trip. I encourage you as I encourage myself to pay close attention to the opportunities presented to you. Living with resentment, hurt and anger promotes wheel spinning and gives your power to a storyteller (your ego) who really doesn't know you. Watch for signs every day and allow your story to evaporate, so that you can invite more of what you want into your life.

Inspired Assignment:

Think of people or situations in your life that cause clutter in your mind. Does the drama of someone else's life take up your time and energy? Does a past hurt run your life? Does it make you afraid to move forward? What stories and what players in your life are not in line with what it is you want to receive? Write about it on the blank pages that follow this chapter.

Know that anything is possible and that you deserve happiness and joy. This is truth; your lack of deserving is the illusion.

Start by noticing the situations that clutter and begin the process of letting go. You can shift the vibration of any situation by listing what you have to be grateful for about that situation. This mindfulness exercise takes the focus off of what is not working and puts it on what is.

Tony Robbins, the inspiring teacher of how to live your life "on purpose," talks about how to take a great idea, add some action to it and get a result. Once you see the outcome, even if it's small, you'll believe in your idea a little more. When you add a little more action, the results grow until your idea has such momentum that it springs to life in a way you could not have planned or, in some cases, imagined.

This is how I believe successful people bring their dreams into reality. It's not enough to have an idea, you have to take action; releasing what it is that holds you back (limiting beliefs about yourself and your circumstances) is part of the plan to get great results!

Our power is not tied to our status, stature or style! Real power lives in the knowing that our past is not in any way controlling our lives; our power is in the present moment.

Surrendering the stories and the clutter in our thinking mind instantly shifts energy and creates an opening for us to receive.

We often can't realize the benefit of the lessons we learn from our teachers until we look back and appreciate that those people were in our path for a purpose, even if it wasn't pleasant at the time.

"We can't solve problems by using the same kind of thinking we used when we created them."

Albert Einstein

The instant we relinquish the story, the vibration begins to shift because our feelings alter and the law of attraction matches our new vibration, bringing new situations and new people to answer our request.

GRACE AND ILLUMINATION

I grew up in a Catholic family where grace was a prayer we said before meals. In our house, it was customarily reserved for special occasions. It went something like, "Bless us, oh Lord, and these, thy gifts, which we are about to receive from thy bounty through Christ our Lord. Amen." I understood it to be a blessing of the food, although I didn't hold that intention when I said the prayer. I simply recited it from memory because that's what was expected. I was focused on the food; I wasn't aware of the power of grace because I didn't really understand what grace was all about.

I have since learned that there are many interpretations of the word grace. The New Testament of the Bible talks about grace as a state of kindness or favour. Some theologians think of grace as the empowering presence of God, enabling us to be who we were created to be. In the Hindu religion, grace is key to achieving self-realization. Dictionary.com defines grace as elegance, beauty of form, manner, motion or action. When we think of a graceful person, we think of someone who moves with ease and refinement.

The words grace and illumination go together for me now. A moment of grace for me is when something unexpected yet perfect happens, something that snaps me into the present moment. I think of moments of grace as miracles – sometimes these tiny miracles are meant just for me and sometimes they are obvious to the world. I believe that these magical moments are intended to remind us that we are on the right track.

Moments of grace illuminate our path, encouraging us, comforting us, showing us that everything is as it should be. Each one of us will have our own experience with grace. It might be a conversation about something that inspires you or a seemingly random meeting with someone who shares some wisdom you need. For some people it's noticing the clock at the same time, it might be thinking of someone and out of the blue they call or something you notice repeatedly, something that becomes a symbol for you.

There are moments of grace in nature when you observe the beauty of the seasons changing or a small animal following its natural instinct. I love to watch the leaves change colour over a few weeks each fall. All around my home, maple trees put on quite a show. Initially it's beautiful and on closer examination it becomes profound, especially when you consider that this is Mother Nature doing her work, creating miracles. Nature is inspiration in action too. When we observe in quiet we become present to the presence of spirit; after all spirit is a part of all activity and thought.

The principles of *Inspiration in Action* are all connected and grace is a fundamental component. When we cultivate a grateful mindset, we have the courage to remember who we really are and we choose to become willing to surrender and release the stories that are not in line with what we want. We invite grace by asking for signs and symbols to light the way, then it's a matter of making ourselves available to receive the messages we need to encourage or comfort us. It's as if we begin to see the world with a fresh perspective, noticing things we had previously overlooked.

One day my husband was in the kitchen and asked me if we had any lemons. I called out from the living room that I had seen one in the fridge. After he stood with the door open, peeking around jars and leftovers, I asked if he needed my help. I went into the kitchen and stood beside him. There in plain view on the top shelf, right up front, in a clear plastic bag was a cut lemon.

I'm not telling you this story to point out anything in particular about my husband, the same situation has happened to me 100 times, as I'm sure it has to you. The very thing you're looking for is right in front of you. We've all heard stories of couples who started out as good friends and after they're married they tell everyone how they couldn't believe that the love of their life was right in front of them. It's amazing how simple miracles seem so extraordinary when we don't expect them.

Since I began this journey of *Inspiration in Action*, I have witnessed countless simple miracles and some pretty big ones too. Evidence of grace is all around us when we are available to experience it.

Love is All Around

I have this thing with hearts now – I see them everywhere. They are attracted to me as I am to them. For a few years, the red tin roof on a log house on the other side of the river from our home appeared to be in the shape of a heart. The tree branches fell in such a way that only from our house and only when the sun was high, the red roof appeared to be a bright red heart. The branches have grown over now and the red heart is a memory I will cherish forever. It was really one of the first big hearts I noticed. I tried to photograph it many times, but my camera couldn't capture what my eye could see. It was like a special secret that only my husband and I knew about.

My attraction to hearts has accelerated since then. They show up in the most unexpected places and almost always at a meaningful moment, as though the Universe is really telling me something, reassuring me.

I thought they were perhaps a message from my late mother, however a wise seer told me that the hearts are a message from the Universe, returning to me that which I am giving out. I think that's pretty cool.

Often on our morning walk, I'll notice heart-shaped stones or stains on the asphalt. They've always been there, I just didn't see them. I can see that hearts have always been around me but until recently, I wasn't really available to notice the message they carried. Now I see them as a gentle reminder that love really is all around us.

Many years ago, my mother gave me a silver heart on a chain. I kept it in a sock in my drawer because at the time I didn't wear much jewelry. When my mother passed away, I took out the heart and wore it almost every day. In a way I felt it was her message to me, saying what she was not capable of saying with words. I cherished that silver heart as a reminder that love trumps everything. As my hurt began to heal, the heart became a symbol of what I really wanted in my life. I wanted less drama and more love.

About three years ago, I went to look for the silver heart and couldn't find it anywhere. It bugged me until I decided that if I'd lost it or left it somewhere, the person who found it likely needed it more than I did at that time. I wasn't happy about losing one of the few pieces of jewelry I owned that had sentimental value, but I did eventually resign myself and put it down to carelessness on my part.

Separate but still related to this tale is another story about the same heart. A dear friend of mine spent the better part of a year dealing with cancer. He was brave; he and his family did everything they could to make him well.

His wife and I made a date for me to go to see him, once they got the news that there was nothing more the medical world could do for him. She called early in the morning on the day of my proposed visit to say that he had had a bad night and wasn't up for my visit. I planned to try again and went out of town for the weekend.

That night, as I was getting ready for bed, I unzipped the side pocket of my cosmetic bag and there was the silver heart on a chain that I thought had been lost. It had been there the whole time. I was blown away by the timing because I felt that my friend was getting close to leaving us. I held on to that heart and I cried. I cried because I was sad, knowing that this heart had come to me as comfort in a difficult time, and I cried for joy because I knew that he would be just fine. This story isn't really about me; it's about the beautiful love intelligence that is all around us, illuminated in experiences of grace, like that one.

Amazing Grace

Here's another heart story about the newest addition to our family, Simon-Oreo. When our calico cat Madison was ready to leave the earth, my husband and I were devastated. If you're a pet owner, I'm sure that you understand the connection we had with this little treasure. Madison wasn't very old, but her little body was no longer serving her and it was our responsibility to let her go. We have another cat, Foster, and thought it would be a good thing to find him a buddy rather quickly. My husband and I went to the Humane Society near us and looked at the cats, but there just wasn't a fit and I decided that it was too tough to go looking.

I put it out there that the cat would show up somehow. That was Friday and by Monday a workmate e-mailed to say that a friend of hers had a kitten that badly needed a new home. Her young daughters were allergic and their hearts were broken. I knew without a doubt that this was our cat. Kensel and I went the next evening to meet Oreo and instantly fell in love with him.

At two months old, he was feisty and adorable. We brought him home that evening and christened him Simon, keeping Oreo as his middle name. We introduced Simon-Oreo to Foster and within a few minutes he was making himself at home. It didn't take long before I noticed that Simon had a black heart on the back of his right leg. Seriously . . . white fur, black heart. When the little girls came to visit Simon-Oreo in his new home, the first thing they did was look for the heart; thankfully they saw it too!

After I gave a presentation to a women's business network recently a few of the guests approached me to share that they see hearts too. One woman was relieved that someone shared her experience. I hope that she sees her hearts as moments of grace and encouragement now. I also have a friend who sees dimes all the time, so often in fact that she started collecting them. Cathy is convinced that they're a special message for her and I believe they are.

Valerie sees pennies and told me that she thinks of a dead relative when she sees them. I believe it is Valerie's moment of grace and an acknowledgement that her departed relative is with her. Valerie also told me that sometimes when she's cleaning out her cat Skittle's litter box, she finds clumps in the shape of a heart.

I asked her to photograph them and send them to me. Why not? I believe that grace is delivered to each of us in a package that we can recognize and humour is always welcome. We don't need to force these magical experiences, we only need to invite them and remain open to receiving the messages they carry.

Grace and illumination are subtle and powerful forces in our lives, if we're available to experience them. I love it when people tell me that they don't believe in miracles. It makes me smile because if they could only appreciate what a miracle it is that they are here, breathing, I'm sure their life would change.

Consider grace like a solar light along your life path. It is charged by your awareness and connectedness to something greater than yourself; it's illuminated when you are mindful and available for the experience.

Inspired Assignment:

Expect miracles; believe in them. Be open to allowing all good to come your way. Train your storyteller by catching yourself and flipping any negative, doubting thoughts to more positive and willing feelings. Then ask to receive and start to look for evidence of grace in your life.

Notice how people will say things that are meaningful for you in some way. Notice how you'll start a conversation with someone and discover that they're a key for something you've been looking for. Notice signs and symbols that will be unique gifts for you. Be willing and open to receiving these powerful messages. They are showing up to tell you something.

Although our thinking mind has trained us to believe it when we see it, the opposite is true: you will see it when you believe it.

Use the blank pages at the end of this chapter to make note of the moments of grace that show up in your life.

Moments of grace illuminate our path, encouraging us, comforting us, showing us that everything is as it should be.

We invite grace by asking for signs and symbols to light the way, then it's a matter of making ourselves available to receive the messages we need to encourage or comfort us.

We don't need to force these magical experiences, we only need to invite them and remain open to receiving the messages they carry.

Compassion and Kindness

Our thinking mind, ego or storyteller would have us believe that we need to judge others in order to feel better about ourselves. Its job is to be a protector, so it stands to reason that no matter what the circumstances are, we need to come out on top. At least that's according to our thinking mind.

What I am learning by reading books like Dr. Jill Bolte Taylor's *My Stroke of Insight* is that the left brain storyteller or ego sees sorting information as its job. Thank the stars for our thinking mind: it's responsible for keeping us on the right side of the road when we drive our car; its job is to remember our name, where we live and our children's birthdays.

It is truly a miracle worker and I appreciate everything the thinking mind is capable of doing for us especially now that I am learning to manage it. When we let the thinking mind run the show, we leave the door open for all kinds of random, silly stuff to invade our lives.

The Course in Miracles, by Dr. Helen Schucman, refers to one tiny mad idea that our ego or storyteller gets hold of and off it goes on some random tangent, making up stories around that one idea. We go along with the show when we don't know any better; when we aren't aware that we are in charge of our thinking mind. Consider the thinking mind like a little two-year-old child. It requires tender, loving discipline.

Be Kind to Yourself First

One of our thinking mind's favourite tasks is judgment. We can be hard on ourselves and on other people – the process is quick and easy, even comfortable for our thinking mind. If you look a certain way, you must be a certain type of person, so I'll file you over here. Our thinking mind likes everything to be organized, so we judge situations and people in order to file them in what we think is an appropriate compartment. It happens hundreds of times each day; we do it automatically, without thinking. There's the key . . . we do it without thinking, without being mindful of what chaos we're creating for ourselves or what damage we might be doing to someone else by simply judging and dismissing them.

Remember that according to the law of attraction what we think about and focus our attention on is what expands in our lives. Judgment brings about more judgment and if it's not on the list of what we want then here's an opportunity to shift focus to something else. When you give your thoughts a second thought, you can see how absurd this judging habit is and how choosing another thought, such as compassion, will bring a different result. I can guarantee that it will be a better outcome for you and for the person to whom you are extending compassion.

I have to say again what an amazing tool our thinking mind is and if managed well, it will serve us well. Where we get into trouble is when we believe everything our thinking mind tells us, including that everything needs to be filed away neatly.

Our thinking mind wants us to believe that we should be in control, however life is so much easier when we give up the perception of control and accept that there is a flow to this life. Our job is to get into that flow.

When we become mindful of the power of the ego or the storyteller and learn to manage it, our need to judge others eases off until it's not required. What we begin to recognize is that we're all connected and judgment separates us. Compassion bubbles up when we recognize that we're all related, as members of this family called the human race, even though our lives may be completely different. We recognize that even though we may appear to be different, we all know joy, we all know suffering and we all feel the same things.

So why would I judge you? Why would I not stand beside you and recognize myself in you and allow you to recognize yourself in me? It takes practice to nurture more compassion and kindness for ourselves and for others. It's one of those mindfulness habits that will shift the energy you're giving off when you catch yourself. It will feel so good to shift a habit that doesn't serve what you want to one that makes you available to receive.

I'm sure you hope that others will have compassion for you when you struggle, so why not give that gift to yourself. Then extend compassion to every single person you encounter in your day. Expect to fall off the path. I often do, however I get back on much quicker and I find that I have more kindness and more compassion available to give to myself and other people as a result.

When we can be tender toward ourselves, we'll begin to see the error in always putting others' needs ahead of our own and we'll start to understand the wisdom in putting our needs first. It may sound selfish to say that you should put yourself first because we women are encouraged to put others' needs ahead of our own. Over time, we can lose ourselves while we're looking after everyone else. Being kind toward ourselves is a great self-care practice and sets a great example for those around us.

We are student and teacher, learning to be tender and compassionate about our own situation with the understanding that everything has something to teach us. In this way, we inspire others to look at themselves with tenderness and compassion.

Taking a Stand

This brings me to the subject of bullying. We can define bullying as intimidation, harassment, victimization or mistreatment. The behaviour is widespread and sometimes subtle, so as not to be acknowledged as bullying. Bullying is happening among people of all ages.

Sometimes we get stuck on the silliest ideas and think that there's power in putting someone else down. What one person thinks is innocent fun can be devastating for someone else. When I was a young girl, people often teased me about being short, but never in a cruel way. It was the most obvious thing about me, so I understand why but I always wished that people could see beyond the fact that I was short. I think that's true for every single one of us. We want to be seen as a person.

My friend Caroline, who is also short in stature, was called "fly shit" when she was growing up. Now that isn't even cute. We talked about that nickname recently and she wondered if that played into her difficulties with self-worth as a child. I can certainly see why she would wonder.

This intimidating behaviour isn't reserved for kids and while we are doing a better job of creating awareness of the behaviour in schools, we haven't addressed how or why they are learning the behaviour. Where we really need to begin to shift this behaviour is with adults, whose behaviour filters down to their children. If kids observe their parents and other adults speaking disrespectfully about other people, they think it's acceptable. If they observe so-called responsible adults mocking others, they think the behaviour is just fine. It's up to each one of us to become the example for other adults and for young people.

Bullying and intimidating others is not okay. Let's look for another way to address where that need comes from. It comes from our thinking mind or ego's need to be right by making someone else less or small or weak or wrong.

Think about the energy of bullying – it's a revved up toxic energy delivered like a one-two punch. Bullying is dangerous and can be lethal behaviour. Bullying is really about the bully and not about the victim, so each of us needs to check our intention when we're making fun of others.

I used to have a razor sharp tongue that could cut through anything. I abused my gift of humour and made fun of other people as a way to make myself feel better. It doesn't work; in fact it works against us. Consider how the law of attraction works: what you think about and focus your attention on is what shows up in your life. If I was focusing on being critical and sarcastic, guess what? That's what was going to come back to me and that's not at all what I wanted.

As I began to withdraw from this behaviour, I noticed that if I was going to shift it out, I was going to have to make some alterations in my life. I seemed naturally drawn to people who were kind and compassionate and started to avoid people who were hurtful with their words either intentionally or unintentionally.

I fall off the wagon with this behaviour too, but again I get out of it much quicker and recognize that no matter who we're talking about everyone needs compassion. We all want and need support and the shift begins with each one of us not tolerating bullying of any kind.

Watch for patterns in your thinking to learn how you can become more loving and kindhearted toward yourself first then toward everyone else. I want to encourage you as I encourage myself to use the power tools of compassion and kindness over judgment and begin the journey of developing more nurturing thinking habits. When we apply these power tools, we are bringing our dreams into clearer focus by removing the barrier of judgment.

Inspired Assignment:

Developing more compassionate thinking takes practice. Start with yourself. Thinking patterns are not fixed in stone. We are in charge of them and with compassion we can shift our thinking habits to produce a better result.

When you feel injured by someone's comment, for example, remind yourself that it's your thinking mind/ego responding and resist the temptation to make someone else wrong about it. Remember that what other people say is a reflection of them and not of who you are. Even if you feel the need to make someone wrong at first, catch yourself and shift the thought to compassion for yourself for feeling that way. Recognizing that it's the thinking mind/ego at work is the first step in shifting the habit. Be kind. The practice is for life and I promise that it gets easier and the reward is worth the effort.

On the blank pages at the end of this chapter, write a list of people you have judged. I mean pivotal people in your life. Reframe your thoughts around those people and call on compassion to help you. Shift your thoughts to kindness and compassion to take the focus off of the barrier that prevents you from receiving. Find a compassionate thought to think even if it's that he or she didn't know better or that their perceived act was about them and not about you. Begin with one person. Start somewhere.

*Consider the thinking mind like a little two-year-old child.
It requires tender, loving discipline.*

Our thinking mind wants us to believe that we should be in control, however life is so much easier when we give up the perception of control and accept that there is a flow to this life.

It will feel so good to shift a habit that doesn't serve what you want to one that makes you available to receive.

*We are student and teacher, learning to be tender
and compassionate about our own situation with the
understanding that everything has something to teach us.*

FORGIVENESS

Forgiveness is one of the most challenging principles of *Inspiration in Action*. There's an expression that goes something like, "hurt people hurt people." It is true that people who live in pain often share it with others.

Let's define forgiveness as the process of letting go: letting go of the thoughts and feelings that keep us in the story of whatever offence we feel was committed against us. Let's adopt Oprah's idea that forgiveness is letting go of the hope that the past could have been any different.

This is not to be confused with forgetting. While the experience will remain in our memory, our feelings about the experience will shift once we choose to embark on the journey of forgiveness. Forgiveness does not dismiss the situation. It simply reframes it so that we can remove the barriers to receiving peace, joy, empowerment, whatever we desire.

Hanging on to past hurt keeps us in the past so that opportunities coming our way today are missed because we're not available to see them. We carry the burden of past hurt sometimes like a badge of honour, when really it is more of a boat anchor keeping us stuck in place.

Let Go of the Illusion

I am a person who has had a lot of forgiving to do in my life and I feel satisfied now that I have found peace with the people and situations that caused me to feel hurt, anger and resentment. Beneath my generally cheery exterior, I struggled with self-esteem issues and suffered over and over every day, as I lived with the illusion that I wasn't enough. It was a message I had been fed by the closest person to me growing up – my mother. I believed her, even though people outside of my family were telling me that I mattered and had an important role to play. Having poor self-esteem led me to make poor choices in relationships. I felt that I wasn't enough, so I tried to fill myself with other people's energy and that plan failed miserably again and again.

Finally in my mid-30s, after having had enough struggling and suffering, I made a choice to move past the pain that was clearly holding me back in my life. I asked for help. A good friend encouraged me to see a therapist and as difficult as it was to make the first appointment, I am so happy now that I did. For me it was a rewarding experience that helped begin my journey of forgiveness.

As it was in my case, sometimes the hurt has been there for so long that we aren't conscious of its source. The hurt can show up in many areas of our lives, such as inappropriate relationships, gambling, serious emotional eating, outbursts of anger and frustration or even bullying behaviour. Holding on to hurt, anger and resentment can manifest as increased stress, anxiety, substance abuse, depression, physical pain and alienation. Scientists are proving that forgiveness can contribute to reversal of these health concerns.

The Journey of Forgiveness

Some people become the star of their sad story and enjoy telling it over and over again. I believe that some of these people want to prevent others from having the same experience, so telling the story becomes a teaching opportunity. However, by telling the story over and over, they are reinforcing the negative impact rather than using forgiveness to shift the outcome for themselves. Using the power tool of forgiveness and then sharing the story of how it empowers us is a more effective message; ultimately, we are teaching by being inspiration in action.

Since each one of us is unique in our life experience, our journey of forgiveness will be unique too. In all cases though, it begins with willingness and necessitates making a choice to shift old beliefs that don't serve what we want. It requires having the courage to investigate the source of our hurt and having compassion for ourselves as we journey through forgiveness.

Think of someone you can trust to listen without judging, such as a doctor, a trusted friend or a spiritual leader, and start investigating your source of hurt or conflict. There is no need to feel either good or bad about the process; just get past what other people think and do it for yourself, so that you can change the outcome in your life.

Know that you can't ask anybody else to change their behaviour. You don't have to let the person you're forgiving know what you're up to. Remain above engaging in negative behaviour if you do communicate with the person you feel hurt you. If you nurture a feeling of empowerment and remain positive, that is what will grow for you.

Be on the path of forgiveness because you want to grow more open to receiving what YOU want. When you do, you will take power away from the story that had a hold on you and you will empower yourself. This power tool is fuelled by compassion, courage and gratitude for the abundance you have in your life and leads to feelings of peace, liberation and hope.

Start with Yourself

The last place we look to find a reason to work on forgiveness is with ourselves. It's a powerful lesson I learned in the process of researching this program.

A little over a year into the study group, I came up with a list of inspired assignments for the women (I call it *The Mindfulness Project* – you'll see a list of tasks in the last chapter of the book). The mission was to carry out the assignment and report back on the outcome at the next meeting.

My third assignment was to "begin the process of forgiving someone." I had to live with that one for a while because I was sure that I had done my forgiveness work. Therapy had helped to start that process and after several years of being mindful of my feelings and consciously letting go of negativity, I felt peaceful where those relationships were concerned. However, there was one person I had not forgiven and I discovered the gift in my assignment.

I opened Doreen Virtue's *Daily Guidance from Your Angels* for inspiration. It's one of those books you can pick up and open to any page.

Here is my message for that day:

Forgive Yourself:
"Ultimately all the resentments that you hold boomerang inward and become self-anger, which percolates to the surface and seeps into your daily life. These feelings can blind you to the everyday joys that await you in the world.

For this reason, we angels are continuously guiding you to release the harmful buildup of resentment in your mind and body. This is the ultimate detoxification that brings you everything you seek: more energy, clearer focus, a greater ability to concentrate, renewed playfulness, love, money . . . you name it. The rewards of forgiveness occur as quickly as light floods a room when a lamp is switched on.

You're much too hard on yourself, beloved one. You believe that perfection is a requirement of being valued, yet you're entirely lovable as you stumble, learn, grow and move on. That's why the most important acts of forgiveness are the ones you direct inward. When you learn to lovingly embrace every part of yourself, the spark within you beams as brightly as a searchlight: healing and attracting others who benefit from your warmth and wisdom.

Release the resentments you have toward yourself today. Let go of any guilt or self-reproach and bathe yourself in much deserved love."

The thought for the day at the bottom of the page is *"I forgive myself and accept that who I am is awesome. I grant myself the same unconditional love that God (universal energy or love intelligence) and the angels give to me. I revel in the delicious feeling of cherishing myself."*

I was blown away by this insight and, while it takes practice to be forgiving, I recognize now that there are no mistakes, only opportunities for learning. I practice releasing resentment because it doesn't belong in my world and it doesn't serve my goals of abundance, beauty, joy, love and peace, prosperity and wellness. I am working on forgiving myself for holding thoughts that don't serve what I want.

It takes a lot of energy to carry around resentment, anger and negativity. The choice is ours when it comes to how we handle misunderstanding, rejection, disagreement or anger. Just keep in mind that it turns on you and the person you're holding those feelings about does not feel a thing. I heard someone say that holding on to anger is like taking a little bit of poison every day and hoping that the other person dies. It just doesn't work; indeed it works against us because ultimately we are poisoning ourselves.

What is that expression about how the best revenge is to get happy? I encourage you to mine your own soul to seek out hidden resentment and anger and to let it go. I encourage you as I encourage myself to be tender and kind toward yourself and to forgive yourself for thinking that you are not enough in some way. You are the pure and perfect manifestation of universal energy on earth. Please don't let your self-criticism and criticism of others keep what you want from showing up in your life. Forgiveness shines a bright light into the darkness and lifts you to a feeling of freedom that you rightfully deserve.

Inspired Assignment:

Each of us will have a unique journey of forgiveness. It begins with the acknowledgement that carrying the burden of anger or resentment toward another person is heavy; it's also a barrier that prevents us from receiving what we want. The journey is about us and not about what any other person may or may not be doing.

Remember the analogy of taking the poison, but expecting the other person to die? Start somewhere. Be willing. Then watch for grace to step in and begin to notice where you're guided to go. By becoming willing to forgive, you instantly shift the energy you have around the situation and you create an opening, so that you can receive guidance.

My journey of forgiveness began many years ago, when a friend had exhausted her good will while listening to me complain about boys. She referred me to the wise psychiatrist who helped me to see that I wasn't really there to complain about boys. I needed to work on forgiving my mother and I needed to work on forgiving myself.

In those sessions, we planted thoughts to replace the ideas that didn't serve my goal of happiness and I began to grow in a different and more authentic direction. I believe that emotional pain is stored in the body and have been guided to investigate homeopathy and various energy healing modalities. I have forgiven what I needed to forgive and I feel blessed to have been guided to meet some incredible people along the way. I believe that you will be guided too if you keep your heart and your mind open and available.

On the blank pages following this chapter, write about areas of your life that require your forgiveness. Begin with yourself. Examine why you need to forgive and begin to release the thoughts that are holding you back from living your best life.

*Forgiveness does not dismiss the situation.
It simply reframes it so that we can remove the barriers
to receiving peace, more joy, empowerment, whatever we desire.*

Be on the path of forgiveness because you want to grow more open to receiving what YOU want.

I heard someone say that holding on to anger is like taking a little bit of poison every day, hoping that the other person dies.

VISION BOARDS

The law of attraction states that when you put your focus on something, you experience more of it. Your vision board will become a powerful tool, reminding you of what you really want. The images and words you choose to put on your board are a clear message to the law of attraction, providing they represent your heart's desire. The process of putting one together is really fun and allows a full connection to and expression of your dreams.

Since you are listening to your soul's desire, it's important that you free your mind of any bias around what other people might think of what you choose. This is your vision after all – not anybody else's. It's important to freely select images and words that really tug at your heart or speak to you in some way. They should reflect of a part of your inner self, waiting to come out.

My first vision board was more like a collage. I put everything I could think of on that board. After living with it for a while, I realized that I already had most of the items on the board in my life, so it was time to revise it. Your vision may shift as you create openings and become more available. As long as the images and words on your board resonate in your heart, they belong there. If something doesn't ring true, simply remove it and wait to be guided so you can unearth new dreams for your life.

Get quiet before you begin creating your vision board and ask for guidance. Be open to receiving inspiration.

Manifesting Miracles

Here's a story from one of my favourite miracle makers about what can be realized when you use a vision board. Michelle Valberg is a world-renowned photographer based in Ottawa, Ontario. She was the first person, aside from my husband, that I discussed starting this project with. She has been my sister, my inspiration, my mentor and my dear friend. In 2006, when the monthly development meetings for the principles of *Inspiration in Action* were wrapping up, I interviewed the women in the group. This is what Michelle had to say:

"When I was developing my vision board there wasn't even a question what I would put on there. I had airplane stickers from my son and when I would look through magazines and I would see a title like, 'This is your year for miracles,' I would cut it out.

There was never a question of what I wanted – I specifically wanted my photographs in National Geographic magazine and I wanted to go to certain places in Northern Canada. I even added a pamphlet about a polar bear expedition that my dad had given me and now I'm preparing for a trip to photograph polar bears.

I had two images of polar bears on my vision board – one of them kissing and one of them standing up – and so far I've seen exactly those two images in person and have now captured them with my camera. I haven't got the cover of National Geographic yet, but I can say that my photograph has been published in the magazine. I also drew the Northwest Passage and Iceland and I have now travelled to both places. Oprah's television show is on the vision board and I have $1,000,000 bill that a friend gave me which I may move around on the board to see if that will help.

My goal has always been to be a world-renowned photographer, but there's this element of success that maybe needs to be redefined. I'm now learning that success comes in a lot of different forms and it's not necessarily through what's in my bank account. In my mind, I have to achieve certain levels in my life to know what success means and then money will follow.

Learning to focus on gratitude for what we already have is like holding out a magnet to the Universe and it's a challenging lesson to get, especially when we doubt our ability and our mission. I sat in Nunavik and stared out at the Universe. I held my arms out wide and I said thank you, thank you, thank you. You can't say thank you enough and through the principles of Inspiration in Action, *I'm reminded of that all the time."*

Six years later, Michelle has been to Canada's North 26 times, she's published a children's book about polar bears and is publishing another book exploring the people, landscape and wildlife of the North called *Arctic Kaleidoscope*. Her images have graced the cover of several magazines, including National Geographic and she has been honoured with awards and accolades from clients, friends and family.

Along her journey the vision has become much clearer. Today she'd tell you that she's connected with her life purpose and is no longer afraid to receive the abundance that comes when we remove the barriers. Michelle works the principles of *Inspiration in Action* and recognizes that all of them take practice to create miracles. Using a vision board supports our dreams and is a visual reminder of what is our heart's desire. Looking at your vision board should feel magical. Believe then receive.

Inspired Assignment:

Creating a vision board is lots of fun and can reveal wisdom you may not be expecting. There are several methods and formats to use when creating a vision board. You can use corkboard and push pins, cardboard or paper and glue. You can find images on the Internet and build a virtual vision board that you can then print and place in a location that you will see often. Do whatever feels comfortable for you.

Magazines are fantastic inspiration for your vision board. Try to have a variety of magazines available to choose images and words and then get into the zone by getting quiet and putting on some soothing music, so that you are available to hear your own inner wisdom.

Notice what images stop you in your tracks, take your breath away or connect with you through some kind of physical reaction. Select these images or words and create a pile. Take your time and enjoy the process. Remember that there is no correct answer and it's not a contest.

Once you have a pile, spread out your paper or corkboard and start attaching the images and words in a way that makes you feel good. You can break up the surface into areas of your life: health, job, relationships or you can place them randomly. Don't feel that you have to use all of the images you selected. Perhaps keep a file with the leftover images in it to either use or discard later.

The trick to creating an effective vision board is in the power of your relationship with the images. Make sure that you feel a strong connection with what's on your vision board. You might consider finding a photograph of yourself that you love and placing it in the centre of your vision board.

I keep my vision board on the wall beside my desk, where I spend most of my time during the day. I like to know that it's close to me while I'm working, reminding me of my dreams. Remember that when you put your focus on something, you experience more of it. Use your vision board as a power tool to help you believe it; then you'll see it!

Your vision may shift as you create openings and become more available. As long as the images and words on your board resonate in your heart, they belong there.

AFFIRMATIONS

Affirmations are agents for change. We're talking about changing a thinking habit. So instead of listening to the left brain analyze everything about you constantly, how about using a tool that will help you shift your thinking to receive more of what you really want out of life.

Affirmations are simple statements of who you are and who you are becoming. They are a shortcut to the truth of who we really are outside of our thinking mind. I use my affirmations when I'm doing challenging poses in yoga or when I'm out on a walk in the country and have to get up a steep hill.

If I didn't use them, my left brain would be having a field day sabotaging my best efforts, telling me that I'm afraid for some reason, that I'm not strong enough to do the pose or that I'm tired. Instead, I use my list of affirmations and push through. I feel more empowered and, as a result, more positive in my life.

Affirmations are a direct plug-in to your spirit. They flip the vibration around you and signal to the law of attraction that you are whatever your affirmations say you are. I have memorized my affirmations and add to the list when I feel guided to do so.

Choose from the following and feel free to add your own. Listen to the whispers and acknowledge the recognition you feel when you read the words. Is there a quality that you want or need in your life? Choose that quality, even if you don't fully understand why. It's not a left brain function, listen to your spirit.

My preference is to use "I am" affirmations and I didn't fully understand why until I heard Dr. Wayne Dyer explain that "I am" is really our connection to who we truly are . . . I am spirit, Universal energy, essence, god force, whatever you call it. "I am" is a declaration and a quick connection to the greater energy we are all part of.

My list of affirmations has grown since I began using them and I expect that it will continue to grow. Feel free to adopt any that resonate with you.

This is me, becoming more of me:
I am able, I am abundant, I am adventurous, I am amazing, I am attractive, I am authentic, I am aware, I am beautiful, I am a billionaire, I am brave, I am brilliant, I am capable, I am clear, I am compassionate, I am confident, I am connected, I am content, I am courageous, I am creative, I am curious, I am empowered, I am empowering, I am enough, I am fearless, I am forgiveness, I am generous, I am gentle, I am graceful, I am gracious, I am grateful, I am happy, I am healthy, I am inspired, I am inspiring, I am joyful, I am kind, I am loving, I am loved, I am a millionaire, I am a miracle, I am optimistic, I am peaceful, I am perfect, I am positive, I am powerful, I am pure, I am responsible, I am rich, I am sacred, I am safe, I am sexy, I am strong, I am successful, I am talented, I am tasteful, I am tender, I am timeless, I am a treasure, I am true, I am wealthy, I am wise, I am worthy.

Here are some additional qualities: honest, funny, empathetic, caring, mindful, humble, reliable, fit, active and supportive. Make them your own and feel free to change any qualities that don't feel right as you work with them. Remember though, you already are all of these qualities because you, like me, are a manifestation of the greater power. Don't let fear stand between whom you "think you are" and who you really are. Use affirmations to push through the fear.

One of our class participants goes through the alphabet and finds a quality to match each letter. It doesn't matter what your system is, this power tool is a great way to quiet your "monkey mind" (another term for your ego) and reinforce dreams with thoughts that take you in the direction you really want to be headed. Our "monkey mind" will keep us stagnant, sometimes even paralyzed with thoughts that we're not good enough or at least it will analyze every situation. It often discourages us from being brave and having the courage to think our way to what we really want. Affirmations, which are essentially positive and empowering messages to our subconscious, will assist each one of us to partner with our wiser selves to become more of who we truly are.

Inspired Assignment:

On the blank pages following this chapter, make a list of affirmations based on what your own inner wisdom tells you that you are. Use the list presented earlier for inspiration and select affirmations that light you up and speak to the highest part of your possibilities. Repeating these affirmations will shift your energy to bring your thoughts more in line with who you are meant to be.

Louise Hay, founder of Hay House Publishing, is really the godmother of affirmations. She believes in the power of positive words and uses affirmations regularly. She encourages people to say their affirmations in front of a mirror or keep the list taped on the wall beside the mirror, so they're seen frequently. I like to memorize mine, so I have them whenever I need them. You can start with one affirmation or focus on one and change it up when you feel guided to do so.

Caroline, one of the members of our original *Inspiration in Action* group, really connected with her list of affirmations and calls on them when she needs a reminder of who she really is.

"I keep mine on my computer screen, taped to the side of the monitor and when I start feeling bad about myself or feel that I've done something wrong in my mind then I go to the affirmations and they remind me of my value."

Listen to your wisdom and you will know exactly how to apply this power tool in your own life.

Affirmations are simple statements of who you are and who you are becoming. They are a shortcut to the truth of who we really are outside of our thinking mind.

Affirmations are a direct plug-in to your spirit.

BOUNDARIES

You've heard the expression, "good fences make for good neighbours," right? Well, that's true in life as well. Good fences make for good neighbours and healthy boundaries make for good relationships. Boundaries say to the world: I value my emotions, my own needs and I am worthy of you honouring me. We value the needs of others and recognize that they are worthy when we respect their boundaries.

Boundaries are there to protect us from having others diminish our value. When we make gratitude our bottom line and turn to courage instead of fear; when we surrender the stories that don't reflect our goals and choose compassion over judgment, we embark on a wonderful journey of connecting with our inner wisdom.

Remember that we tell people how to treat us through our actions and our words. Consider boundaries as friendly fences and start to visualize using them to protect yourself. It's not a defensive protection like the negative energy that comes from our thinking mind. It's guarding something precious so that it will become even more beautiful.

I used to have weak boundaries. I naively thought that other people would automatically know what was best for me and act in a respectful manner. I didn't understand that other people were working at getting their needs met too and in that process my needs might not be considered. I also didn't recognize that because my boundaries were weak to none, I might be trespassing on other people's property.

It all came to light when I began to focus on what I really wanted. If I wanted peace then stepping into other people's drama would not help me to achieve peace. If I wanted to have peace, I had to think and speak peace. I had to learn to respect that other people see the world differently and there's plenty of room for everyone's perspective.

Now I do my best to keep my views to myself unless someone asks and I let my words and actions stand as an example of what's possible. Setting boundaries requires practice like the other principles of *Inspiration in Action*. So start somewhere and lovingly say no thank you to whatever isn't in line with what you want.

If I value myself, then I need to practice good self-care. If I take good care of myself then I can help you with whatever I have spilling over in my self-care account. If I don't have enough worthiness in my heart then I need to work on that before I can give to you. Many of us give at the risk of our own physical and mental health. We provide a much better model for others when we take care of ourselves first by having healthy boundaries.

If we lovingly set limits on behaviour in our relationships then people will know how far to go. We may have to remind them where the line is and if they can't respect the boundary then it's time to either alter or eliminate the relationship. I have found that some friendships have been strengthened in this process and others simply drift away.

Creating healthy boundaries was a big lesson for a real estate agent we'll call Kelly. Her brother was moving back to town and asked Kelly to help him look for a house. At first, Kelly bristled at the notion that she would be in this situation with her brother because their relationship was such that she would feel uncomfortable.

As soon as Kelly recognized this discomfort, she began to set a boundary around the relationship with her brother. She made a choice to deal with him as she would any other client. This way there was protection from any criticism her brother might have of how Kelly does business and she was free to behave as she would with any of her clients.

Free with compliments and questions, Kelly was able to deliver a great result. She wasn't stuck in any traps that might have been set for her had she dealt with her brother instead of her client. Kelly successfully separated the emotional and the professional with a healthy boundary.

When we're sensitive to other people's needs and act in a respectful manner toward them, we are sending the message that we value them and acknowledge their worthiness. Having healthy boundaries and acknowledging them in others is a key element of *Inspiration in Action* because we are recognizing our worthiness to receive what it is we want.

As we put boundaries in place, we are signaling to both the law of attraction and that power greater than ourselves that we are available to receive because we are focusing on what we really want and clearing the way to accept it. Weak boundaries signal that we're not quite ready.

Protect Your Property

Once we make the choice to put boundaries in place, how do we go forward in our relationship with the person on the other side of the fence? I learned years ago how to deliver what my husband calls a "shit sandwich." It's a fantastic tool that I use all the time when I have to approach delicate subjects, such as people overstepping my boundaries.

The sandwich is made up of three elements: say something positive, follow with the message you need to deliver about how the person overstepped and close with something positive to complete the sandwich. The person will get the message and you'll feel good about delivering it with kindness and compassion.

Let's say that you're a retired person and want to support your children by being a caregiver for your grandchildren. It's important to know where you want to set the boundaries in this situation. If you're seen as a free babysitter then there will be an imbalance because you're allowing someone to take you for granted.

Create a win-win situation by stating up front where the boundary is for you. Be clear about how much time you want to devote to helping care for your grandchildren. You're entitled to a full life and need to ensure that you get your own needs met first. You can then give from your overflow, which in this case is whatever time you have available after taking care of yourself first.

When you speak with your daughter or son, try using the above formula. For example, "I am so honoured that you are comfortable to ask me to help take care of the children. I would be happy to help out every second Tuesday, if that works for you. I have commitments that I need to attend to (no need to explain what they are) so I won't be able to take care of the little loves every week. I hope that you understand that I want to help however I can. Give it some thought and let me know if you want to take me up on my offer."

Too often we fall into patterns in relationships. It's never too late to put boundaries in place and continue to have a productive rapport. It takes courage and love, so use those tools to improve your own situation. Be an inspiration to others by honouring your own wellbeing, making choices that get your needs met first. Then you'll be in a position to offer your goodness to others.

Give from what flows over the top of your well, but be careful not to let others drain it. When we understand what is important in our own lives, it's much easier to say yes to our own goals and no to those who would take our goodness.

Inspired Assignment:

I strongly suggest that you use the blank pages at the end of this chapter to write down areas of your life where you feel taken advantage of or where you take advantage; where you feel controlled or where you feel the need to control. These are the areas where boundaries should be put in place.

Think of the people who would be on the other side of your boundary and use your imagination to place a beautiful white picket fence, lovingly and with compassion, between yourself and these people (maybe for you it has to be a wall instead). The boundary is now in place. It can be moved back and forth, depending on how your relationship is going. Just make sure to move it wherever it needs to be in order to feel protected. Don't forget to have compassion for the person on the other side of the boundary.

Doing this exercise is the first step in practicing healthy boundaries. Listen to how you're guided to proceed and remember what the flight attendant always says before a flight: place the oxygen mask on yourself first before assisting anyone else. Having healthy boundaries instantly shifts the energy around our thoughts about our relationships and when we make a shift, it's as though the whole world does too. It might feel uncomfortable and that's okay. Be with the feeling and remind yourself that you are doing this for your own good and ultimately for the good of all your relationships.

*Consider boundaries as friendly fences and start to
visualize using them to protect yourself.*

Be an inspiration to others by honouring your own wellbeing, making choices that get your needs met first. Then you'll be in a position to offer your goodness to others.

Many of us give at the risk of our own physical and mental health. We provide a much better model for others when we take care of ourselves first.

THE MINDFULNESS PROJECT

When you do for others, you do for yourself. People who are labeled as "givers" acknowledge that they get as much, if not more, good stuff in the process of helping others. While we should always give from our overflow, finding a way to do simple, thoughtful acts for other people signals to the law of attraction that we have an abundance of something and are available to share and receive more.

If there's something you want to receive, find a way to give it to someone else. Give compliments freely; tell people what you like about them and watch how the world responds to your shift of energy. Remember to be gracious when receiving compliments too.

It's important to fill your own tank with small acts of self-care. If you need a day to yourself, find a family member or friend to assist in making that happen. Perhaps you need to give yourself a gift every day: it can be a small reward and it doesn't have to cost money. How about soaking in a bath tub or reserving an amount of time to read? Give to yourself so that you know what it feels like to receive too.

My ultimate goal with *Inspiration in Action* is to change the world, one inspired act at a time. During a presentation for a local Women's Business Network, I focused on four of the principles in this book; I also wanted to share *The Mindfulness Project* to inspire these powerful business women to share more of themselves with others. I asked my friend Rachel, a talented jewelry maker (www.taikknots.com) to package five bags with two pair of earrings inside each bag. Before the presentation, she randomly handed the gifts out to five women she didn't know in the audience and instructed them to hang on to them until later.

I explained that the exercises in *The Mindfulness Project* are about completing the cycle of giving and receiving and cited a few examples from the list that you will see a little later. Then I mentioned the earrings and asked the women who received the gifts to keep one pair of earrings as a present from Rachel and me; the other pair was to be given to someone in the audience they didn't know. I asked them to notice how it felt to give and receive a gift for no reason in order to show them the power in a small mindful act.

What happened next no doubt changed a few lives. Two member businesses had been featured that evening and after my presentation, they were invited up to announce the winners of a draw featuring a gift from each of them. Then the emcee asked if anyone else in the room wanted to give something away. By the time we finished some 45 minutes later, the energy in the room was palpable and positive. Someone joked that it reminded them of the day Oprah gave everyone in her audience a car. Of the 60 or so people in the room, 18 businesswomen had given a gift to someone in the room. It was pure magic and clear evidence of what I know to be true.

We're all capable of doing something kind for someone else. After drawing up a list of inspired assignments, I asked the women in the *Inspiration in Action* development group to take on a task that was selected randomly from the list and report back on what happened in the following month's meeting.

The assignments are as simple as smiling at three people or buying someone a cup of coffee. It's what the inspired women in the group did with their assignments that blew my mind and moved me to expand the list and include it in this book. Using mindfulness is an excellent exercise; I guarantee that you will give and receive joy and gratitude in the process of completing these assignments. You will feel so good being *Inspiration in Action*.

Here are a few examples of what happened to some of the women in the development group.

Dee was charged with buying someone a cup of coffee and after giving it much thought, she went to the cafeteria in her workplace and gave the owner a $20 bill. She asked him to give away coffee until the money was gone and not to tell anybody who was paying for it. The gentleman who owned the cafeteria often did random acts of kindness himself. He was so happy to tell people that the coffee was free and it was another customer who was paying for it. So with her act of kindness, Dee touched 21 people. Amazing, isn't it?

She shared her results with me a few weeks after we had received our assignments and it inspired me to do more as well. I also sent out an e-mail to the rest of the women in our group and inspired them to do more. You can see how powerful this sort of activity becomes when so much joy comes from doing something simple and thoughtful for someone else.

Here's what Catherine, another member of the development group said:

"I loved the assignments because they were motivating. Something you might previously have thought of, like buying a coffee for the car behind you in the drive-through. You might not have thought it was important, but that person could be having a terrible day or they could be broke. You don't know what kind of difference you can make.

The assignments really helped show me that the little things we can do every day in the world can have an effect on someone else's life. It was nice because we wanted to do our assignments, so it sort of forced us to do those things we thought were meaningless and see how meaningful they actually can be. Being mindful of doing those little things, that's Inspiration in Action.

I hope that most of the time I am a thoughtful person, concerned about other people's feelings, I hope that I address situations so that the outcome is in line with what I want. I am certainly more focused on how I will get there now and I am aware that I can direct my energy, thoughts and feelings to create an outcome. I also realize that when I don't use this mindfulness, when I don't choose my thoughts wisely, the energy just scatters. It sounds so cliché, but if you really put your mind to it you can make anything happen."

In the fall of 2012, I started teaching *The Course in Happiness*, which is based on the eight principles in this book. To help the women in the class get acquainted with *The Mindfulness Project*, I asked them to write a note to someone they appreciated. It could be someone they knew or someone they admired. I gave them the cards to do the assignment and here are a few of the fantastic results.

Although Kathy wasn't subscribing to newspaper delivery, she noticed the middle-aged couple who delivered the paper along her street were out there in the dark, no matter the weather, and decided to write them a thank you note. She taped it to a post so they would see it. Not only did they appreciate it, they wrote her a thank you note in return.

Lindsey noticed a woman at the drive-through coffee place she frequents who is always helpful and happy. She wrote her a thank you note and included a few lottery tickets in the envelope. She left the card anonymously in the comment box.

I wrote an anonymous note to a resident of the town I live in, who has a beautiful border garden that I have admired for over 20 years. I wrote him on behalf of his neighbours to thank him for cultivating beauty in his garden. I put it under his windshield wiper and now when I drive by his house I smile, knowing how good he must feel having received that gift.

Here is a list of other inspired assignments. Try them and see how you feel.

Open a door for a stranger.

Smile at three people you don't know.

Pay for someone else's coffee.

Send an e-mail or a handwritten note to someone, telling them what you appreciate about them. It can be someone you know or don't know. You can sign it or send it anonymously.

Bake or purchase cookies or a treat and deliver them to someone who would not expect it.

Phone two people you haven't connected with in a long time. Have no agenda except to ask how they are.

Make a donation of your time or money no matter the amount. Give to a person or organization that needs support.

Find a good quality in someone you don't like and focus your thoughts on that.

Look through your clothes and find something you don't wear anymore. Give it to someone who needs it more than you do.

Spend a few minutes focusing on your breathing . . . breathe in and breathe out. Relax and breathe.

Do something nice for a neighbour.

Think of someone you know who is overwhelmed by their life. Give them whatever is overflowing in your life: food, money, time, love; whatever you have in abundance.

Give someone you don't know a compliment.

Listen to a friend, a co-worker or even a stranger; listen to what they are saying. Don't offer an opinion or advice unless they ask. Just listen.

Listen to the birds sing – and really hear them sing. At first it will be a pleasant sound, but as you reflect on what is going on you will realize that you are part of something truly amazing. It will be profound and you will begin to hear birds differently.

Find an old photograph of a family member or friend and send it to them in a card with a message full of love.

Thank a friend for being in your life or for inspiring you in some way.

Send someone flowers for no reason.

Spend some time in the most beautiful place you know of in nature. Observe what is around you, listen to the sounds and acknowledge the gift of the present moment.

Be mindful of using kindness in every conversation you have for one day. Acknowledge how that feels.

For one day, acknowledge everyone you can by name, even if it means reading a nameplate or asking for the person's name.

If you're in the habit of bringing your lunch to work, bring an extra meal for someone in your workplace.

Say I love you often.

Bring flowers home for your husband or wife or send them to his or her workplace.

If you're not in a relationship, buy flowers for yourself; feel the beauty and the love for yourself.

Make the time to visit an elderly friend who has difficulty getting out and about. It could be to shop for them, to just drop in for a cup of tea or to bring them a meal. If you don't know anyone in this situation, ask among your friends or call a senior's residence. There are many seniors who don't have any visitors.

Do something for someone who is responsible for the care of a sick relative. Life can be difficult and overwhelming for the family member; they will appreciate the support.

Make sure to say thank you to anyone who gives you good service. Let them know that you appreciate them by sending a note directly to them or to their supervisor, boss or business owner. Get to know the power of thank you.

Make a handmade gift for someone. Bake, knit, sew, crochet, paint or write. Give the gift of love by whatever means you choose to express yourself.

Think of someone who bugs you and search for one quality you admire about them. Give that person a compliment or do something nice for them. You can do it anonymously or not.

Donate food, money or your time to a local food distribution centre, community kitchen or shelter.

Purchase $5 food gift cards and give them to someone who you recognize needs some help. It can be someone you know or a donation to an organization that helps needy people in your community.

Take one day and be mindful of looking everyone in the eye. Smile when you speak with everyone; notice how making this small adjustment makes you feel.

Spend the day noticing beauty: beauty in nature, beauty in yourself and other people, beauty in art and music. Listen for beauty in the words of other people; offer beauty in your words.

Use your Facebook status to state what you're grateful for or what inspires you.

Notice your conversations with others for one day. Be mindful of the temptation to share your stories instead of listening to someone else's.

Unless you are asked, try to be a witness to other people's lives without always putting yourself in the conversation for one day. Be mindful of the inclination to compete with or to outdo someone else. *Inspiration in Action* is listening without having to speak. Wait for someone to ask you a question, which is your cue to share. Be mindful of how often you ask questions of others.

When we share inspiration through our thoughts and our actions, we alter the energy in our world. Do your best to be inspiration in action and resist the temptation to tell people about your inspired acts. Let them be your whispers to the Universe that say "I am available to receive."

I encourage you as I encourage myself to practice shifting your thinking, so that you will be more available to receive what is your heart's desire. Practice gratitude by writing about what you're grateful for until it becomes an easy habit. Be courageous as you plug into the beautiful divine energy that defines your true self and nurtures your dreams. Surrender the stories that aren't in line with your heart's desire. Notice moments of grace showing up as coincidences and believe that they are sent as special messages for you. Soon you'll see that they're not coincidences, they're actually miracles and you'll come to expect them. Practice compassion, kindness and forgiveness for yourself and others. Set healthy boundaries to protect your life's precious mission and be mindful of sharing yourself with others. When we choose happiness over any of the other options our thinking mind offers in a day, we benefit and we model for others what it looks like to be inspiration in action.

If there's something you want to receive, find a way to give it to someone else.

My ultimate goal with Inspiration in Action *is to change the world, one inspired act at a time.*

Sharing Inspiration in Action

When we practice the principles of *Inspiration in Action*, our thoughts and feelings begin to shift; it's as though the world around us shifts as well.

Here are some comments from the women in the development group about how using the power tools of *Inspiration in Action* impacted their lives.

Catherine:

I think the really big shift for me in all of this has been in the day to day. I am very mindful of how I treat people and how they treat me. It's definitely the little things that are helping me to grow as a person.

Terry:

I'm passionate about making the world a better place and in that, I want to make me better. What stands out for me is the use of the words grace, forgiveness, and mindfulness. I've been working on that for a zillion years, but I've been working on it to give other people. This time I worked on it to give myself, so that was really important to me.

I was always aware of being kind toward other people, not kind to myself. I was always forgiving you, not forgiving me. I was always chastising myself if I wasn't giving you what you needed. This time I worked on giving me what I needed. As a result, I am more peaceful.

I really see this process as contributing to a tipping point, changing the mass consciousness one by one, group by group, inspired assignment by inspired assignment – that's the goal.

Having these tools in my life, I see that my relationships are more peaceful. I'm less reactionary. You don't know where to ever give credit for why things change or how you evolve because it's always so many things, but I can honestly say that Inspiration in Action *played a part in that. I'm just more peaceful, kind of like after you meditate. I would come out of a meeting and I would have that peace.*

Caroline:

When Kathie introduced me to the idea of this group, she described it as a group of women who would be exploring how they could make a difference in the world; how they could help others and help themselves. That idea really appealed to me.

I think I've learned to treat myself a lot better and to have more trust and more knowledge of myself. Perhaps that sounds a little selfish, but in many ways I've always been a giving person. Raising two sons, I learned to put them and everyone else first, so I needed to learn how to give to myself and I'm very proud of the fact that I now do that. I think because I now give to myself, it's also changed the relationships I have because when you give to yourself you have more energy to give to others and it's not at a sacrifice.

There were times when I would drive my half hour home after our meetings and I would be completely dumbfounded at what I had learned and how the stories of the women I had spent the evening with resonated with me.

The assignments from The Mindfulness Project *were totally bizarre in that they seemed simple on paper. While I did them, I sort of dismissed their relevance until I realized that there was a lot more meaning in the assignment and its specific relevance for me.*

The example I recall off hand was the assignment where I was supposed to open a door for a stranger. I opened doors when I went to the mall and people smiled and I smiled back, but I had always had a big problem with circumstances that had changed where I live. We used to have a beautiful view of nature from our back deck until someone built a big house that marred the view. To me, that house altered my life; my view on the world had changed and for a few years I resented the people who lived there. I hadn't even met them but I resented them.

The summer I was working on my assignment, I realized who I actually had to open a door for, so I went to the house and introduced myself. After I left, I realized that it was only a house and people had to have a place to live. It was as though a burden had been lifted from my life; I had opened the door for a stranger.

The one word that was used when we first came together was inspiration and it means many things to me. It can mean listening to a co-worker, even when you don't like them. It can mean doing volunteer work even when you're really, really tired. It can mean treating your family in ways you hadn't done before but you're inspired to do it because you know that if you change your attitude, it will make a difference. Inspiration and making a difference are what I keep with me on a day-to-day basis.

Rachel:

For me, Inspiration in Action *has been a slow sort of marinating process. You know how you learn things, but you don't know where you can apply it until an experience happens? I feel that now I'm able to be more mindful in situations; there's an awareness I have now that I didn't have before. It's hard to explain because it's more of a feeling than a thought.*

There is more mindfulness for me around other people. I'm always asking how I can do more for people.

Here's one recent example: I have a friend who was being considered for a new job. Her potential boss called me as a reference and asked me what Alison's worst quality was. I had to think about it because I think Alison is a great girl. I had to come up with something, so I said I don't think Alison values herself as much as other people value her. Isn't that how a lot of people feel about themselves?

Around the same time, I invited Alison to the book launch Peggy McColl was having for her book The One Thing. *The inspiring guest speaker was Bob Proctor and I thought about my friend because I know how much* Inspiration in Action *has helped me and I wanted her to have a taste of that because you never know what little thing will impact someone's life.*

When we left, Alison turned to me and she said she saw herself in what Bob Proctor was talking about and it made her want to do better. She had accepted this new job, but it wasn't honouring who she really is. My friend realized that she had undervalued herself by accepting a position that was not enough for her: not enough of a challenge; not enough of a result. It didn't take long before Alison found a new job with more challenge and greater reward, earning 25% more money than she was earning previously, which has made a significant difference in her life and it goes back to an inspired act. I am grateful that I had the mindfulness to take her to the event and grateful also that she had the courage to make the changes she needed to make in her own life.

Delma:

For me one of the great lessons is learning to set boundaries when you need to. It's not an easy thing to do, but I think in the long run it's really necessary when you're on this journey and you're focused on a good outcome. So I've had to put some boundaries around a relationship in my life and I find that my life is better because of it. The relationship is what it is, but the boundaries help to protect me when I need it. Boundaries are a habit, like all of the principles in Inspiration in Action. *I think I've now developed a really good habit of being mindful, but I still have to really work at it because they're not engrained yet.*

I thought The Mindfulness Project *was great. When you get so busy and caught up in your life, it's a great reminder to stop and do something for someone else. It's so easy to do and the fact that people on the other end are not expecting it makes it a real gift for them. It's a gift for you to see how happy they are.*

Michelle:

The first time I ever had a conversation with somebody about the law of attraction, I didn't know what she was talking about. She said, "Michelle, just keep asking the Universe for what you want; just keep asking for it in a very positive way." She then explained that you can attract what you want with your thinking. I remember that conversation so clearly, I remember where we were and I remember that I didn't want to leave; I wanted to know more. That was my first introduction to the knowing that our thoughts are powerful.

Through Inspiration in Action, *I've learned a lot about having the courage to make changes in relationships that either were unhealthy or were not in line with what I really want in my life. I am learning about having boundaries in relationships so that I can be true to myself, knowing that it doesn't matter what anybody else thinks. If it is a friend or a family member, they are who they are; I know that I can't change that.*

So I am learning to protect myself and believe in what is right for me. It's challenging to use the power tool, knowing that it's never intended to hurt anybody else. The way I see it now, boundaries are necessary to protect my heart and to help me bring my dreams into the light. I recognize that nobody can manifest my dreams, so it's important to be clear with myself about what works and what doesn't in relationships, both professionally and personally.

When you use boundaries and free yourself of negativity, how you rise up!

So far, everything is showing up because I know I have the power to make it happen. It's taken a long time for that power to become real to me and if it doesn't happen, I know there's a reason for it. There's always a reason.

I've learned that when I want something, I go for it, especially when I'm told I can't have it. I tend to want it more and ask for it more.

My passion today, aside from my family, is the North, and I really try to be mindful of appreciating every second of the experience when I'm there. I try to feel the land from my toes up, recognizing how much we receive from nature. I am so excited and honoured to have the opportunity to share the world we live in through my photography.

There's something very powerful in the practice of operating with mindfulness: the more we work with this awareness, the more our awareness of it grows. When we do something for someone else intentionally without expecting anything in return, we are opening ourselves to receiving miracles. Remember the world is an abundant place and we have much to share.

I invite you to connect with the whispers of your heart and to unwrap the divine gifts you've been given. May your journey be filled with the richness and happiness you deserve. Believe and receive.

Kathie Donovan

Acknowledgements

I am deeply grateful to a long list of magnificent people who have shared the journey.

The love of my life: marketing guru, coach extraordinaire, piano man and poet Kensel Tracy, who has been enthusiastic and motivating while offering gentle encouragement and steadfast support.

My family who inspires me and loves me just the way I am. Michelle Valberg who has shared every step of the journey, knowing it would be as beautiful as it has been. Kristin Harold, the best editor in the world, who always offers honest feedback and who has been my best skeptic. Edie Wawrychuk has done a brilliant job of designing the book and has been generous with her sage advice; Tina Tyrell has been my beautiful guardian angel getting this book to print.

The women in the development group who boarded the train with me in the beginning and stayed on board for every stop. My friends, all of you, for being the best friends a girl could ask for.

Kate Mensour, my agent and dear friend, who inspires me with her courage and compassion. Max Keeping always encouraged me to believe in the power of my dreams; his advice has become my creed. Princess and BB, thank you for your love and your mad writing skills. I am also grateful for the students of *The Course in Happiness*, especially the early adopters, who gave wings to these words, as though they were magic.

Thank you Oprah Winfrey, Dr. Wayne Dyer, Louise Hay, Cheryl Richardson, Marianne Williamson, Michael Holden, Mike Dooley and Geneen Roth for teaching me that happiness is the way.

Thank you to Hay House Publishing for permitting me to use an excerpt from Doreen Virtue's book: *Daily Guidance from Your Angels 365 Angelic Messages to Soothe, Heal and Open Your Heart*. Copyright 2006 Doreen Virtue. Hay House, Inc., Carlsbad, CA.

Thank you to Michelle Valberg of Valberg Imaging (www.valbergimaging.com) for inspiring cover photographs.

Thank you to hair wizards Lucy and Kevin at Fluid Colour Concept Salon and to Leslie Anne Barrett for make-up.

Contact Information

Please visit the website to find out about *The Course in Happiness*, based on the principles in this book. To sign up for special events and to contact Kathie Donovan, go to: **www.kathiedonovan.com.**

If a telephone is more your style, you can reach Kathie Donovan for inquiries about *The Course in Happiness* by calling 1-877-718-4869.

To book Kathie for a speaking engagement, contact The Mensour Agency: **www.mensour.ca.**

Manufactured by Amazon.ca
Acheson, AB